The Afternoon Pianist

This publication is not authorised for sale in the
United States of America and/or Canada.

Order No. AM971278

This title was previously published as
Chord By Chord, books 1,2 & 3

Cover design by Chloë Alexander
Photograph courtesy of Images Colour Library

Printed in EU.

ISBN 978-0-7119-8964-8

Visit Hal Leonard Online at
www.halleonard.com

World headquarters, contact:
Hal Leonard
7777 West Bluemound Road
Milwaukee, WI 53213
Email: info@halleonard.com

In Europe, contact:
Hal Leonard Europe Limited
42 Wigmore Street
Marylebone, London, W1U 2RY
Email: info@halleonardeurope.com

In Australia, contact:
Hal Leonard Australia Pty. Ltd.
4 Lentara Court
Cheltenham, Victoria, 3192 Australia
Email: info@halleonard.com.au

CD Track Listing

1. Eight Days A Week
Words & music by John Lennon & Paul McCartney
Northern Songs/ATV Music

2. One More Night
Words & music by Phil Collins
Hit & Run Music (Publishing) Limited

3. Massachusetts
Words & music by Barry Gibb, Robin Gibb & Maurice Gibb
BMG Music Publishing Limited

4. Release Me
Words & music by Eddie Miller, Dub Williams & Robert Yount
Acuff-Rose Music Limited

5. La Bamba
Adapted and arranged by Ritchie Valens
Carlin Music Corporation

6. The Sound Of Silence
Words & music by Paul Simon
Pattern Music Limited

7. Top Of The World
Words by John Bettis, music by Richard Carpenter
Rondor Music (London) Limited

8. Wonderful Tonight
Words & music by Eric Clapton
Warner Chappell Music Limited

9. Super Trouper
Words & music by Benny Andersson & Bjorn Ulvaeus
Bocu Music Limited

10. Scarborough Fair/Canticle
Arrangements & original counter melody by Paul Simon & Art Garfunkel
Pattern Music Limited

11. Sailing
Words & music by Gavin Sutherland
Island Music Limited

12. The Lady In Red
Words & music by Chris be Burgh
Rondor Music (London) Limited

13. Guantanamera
Words by Jose Marti, music adaptation by Hector Angulo & Pete Seeger
Harmony Music Limited

14. There Goes My Everything
Words & music by Dallas Frazier
Acuff-Rose Music Limited, London W1

15. Anniversary Song
Words & music by Al Jolson & Saul Chaplin
Campbell Connelly & Company Limited

16. Green Green Grass Of Home
Words & music by Curly Putman
Burlington Music Company Limited

17. One Moment In Time
Words & music by Albert Hammond & John Bettis
Windswept Pacific Music Limited/Warner Chappell Music Limited

18. Imagine
Words & music by John Lennon
BMG Music Publishing Limited

19. By The Time I Get To Phoenix
Words & music by Jim Webb
Island Music Limited/EMI Songs Limited

20. (Everything I Do) I Do It For You
Words by Bryan Adams & Robert John 'Mutt' Lange, music by Michael Kamen
Rondor Music (London) Limited/Zomba Music Publishers Limited/MCA Music Limited

21. Your Cheatin' Heart
Words & music by Hank Williams
Acuff-Rose Music Limited

22. Ob-La-Di, Ob-La-Da
Words & music by John Lennon & Paul McCartney
Northern Songs/ATV Music

23. Rock Around The Clock
Words & music by Max C. Freedman Jimmy de Knight
Myers Music Limited

Eight Days A Week

Words & Music by John Lennon & Paul McCartney

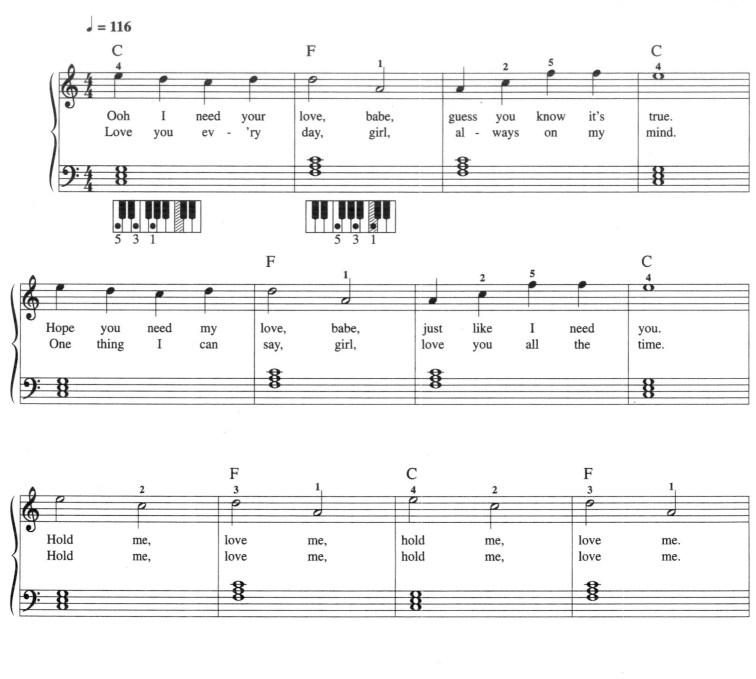

One More Night

Words & Music by Phil Collins

Massachusetts

Words & Music by Barry Gibb, Robin Gibb & Maurice Gibb

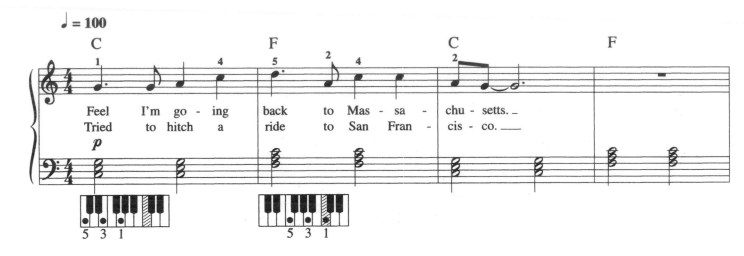

Release Me

Words & Music by Eddie Miller, Dub Williams & Robert Yount

La Bamba

Adapted & Arranged by Ritchie Valens

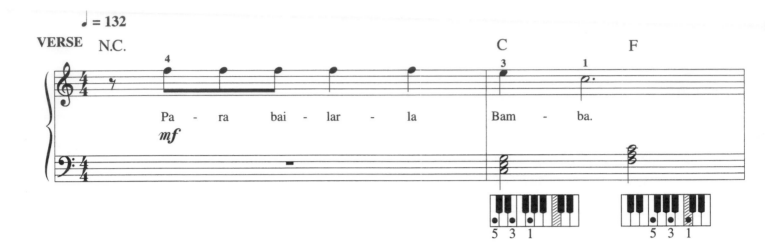

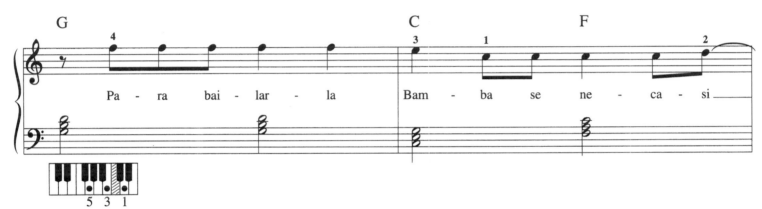

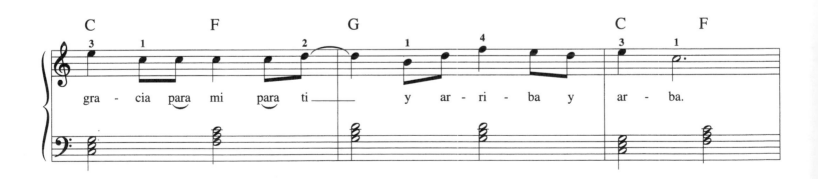

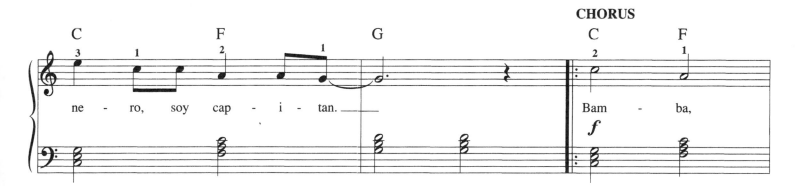

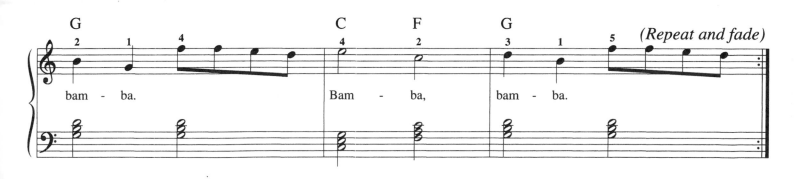

The Sound Of Silence

Words & Music by Paul Simon

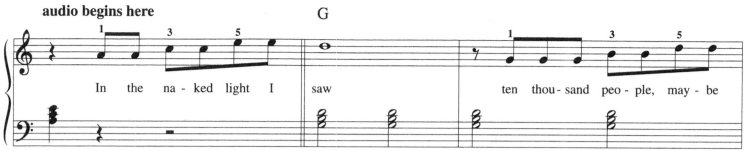

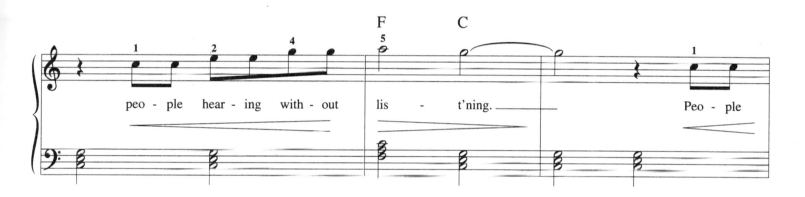

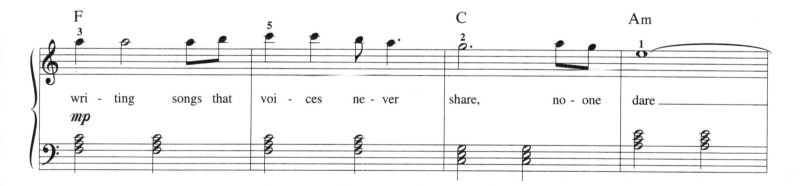

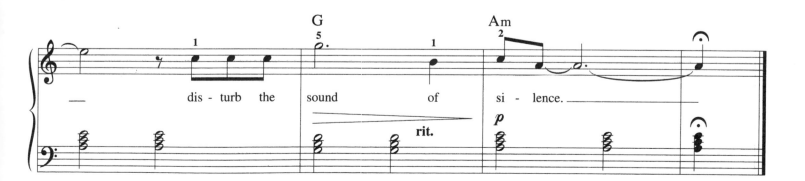

Top Of The World

Words by John Bettis.
Music by Richard Carpenter

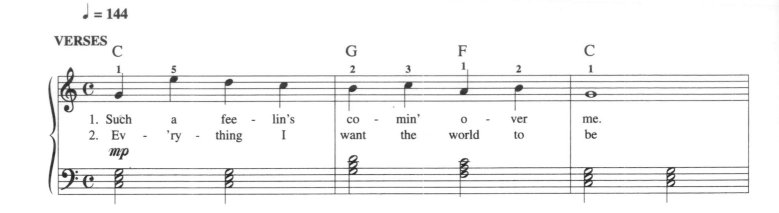

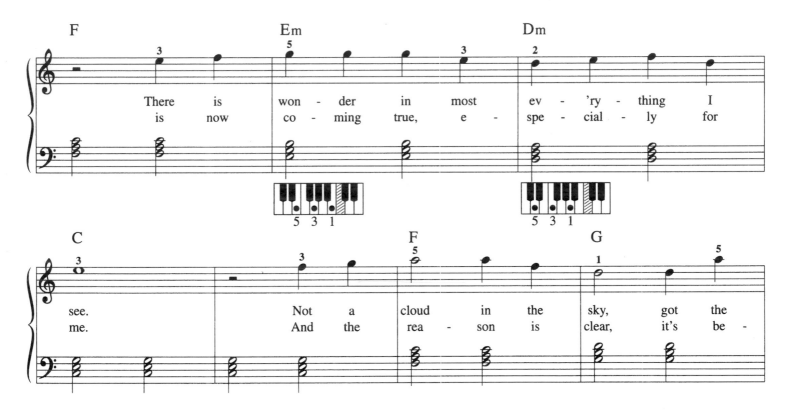

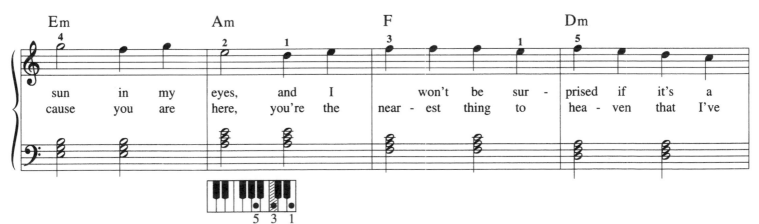

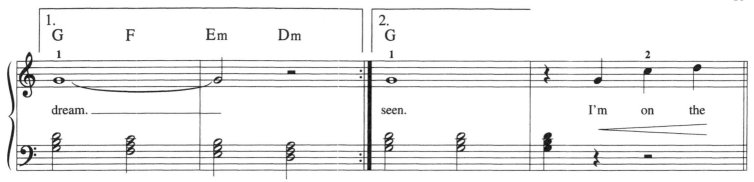

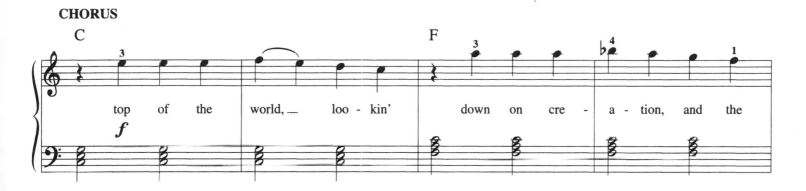

CHORUS

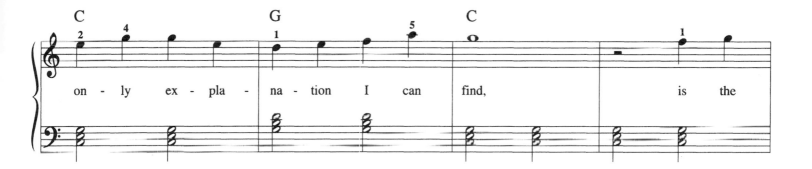

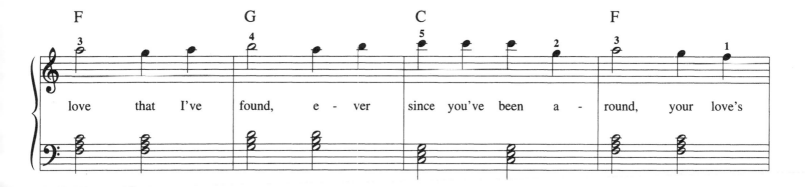

Wonderful Tonight

Words & Music by Eric Clapton

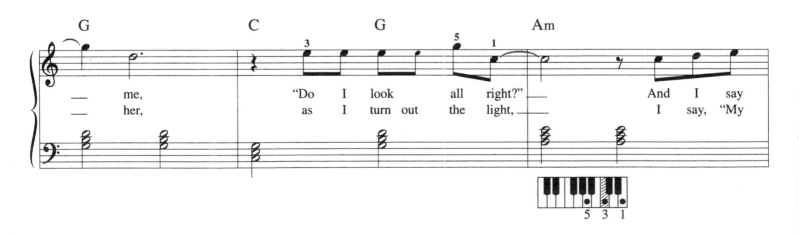

15

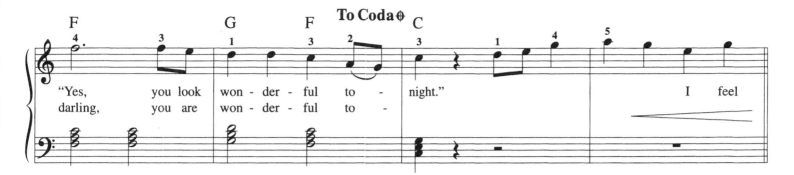

INTERLUDE

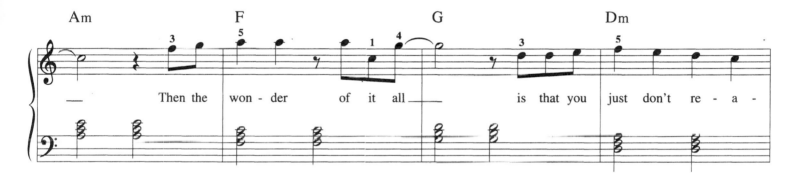

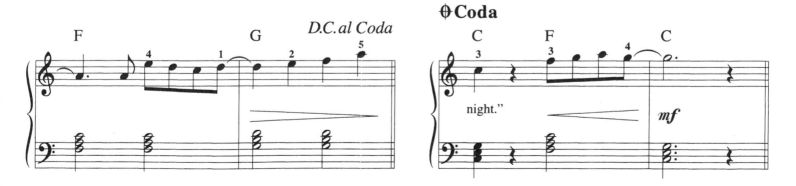

Super Trouper

Words & Music by Benny Andersson & Bjorn Ulvaeus

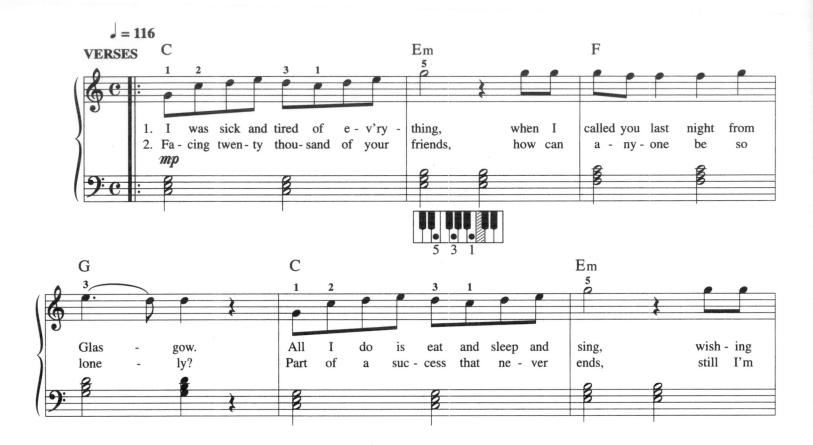

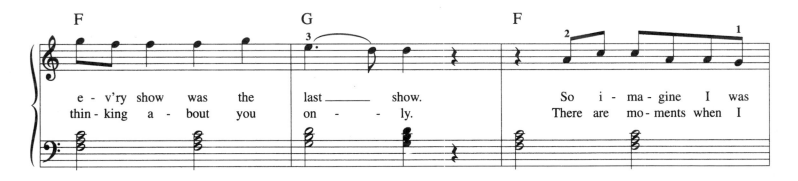

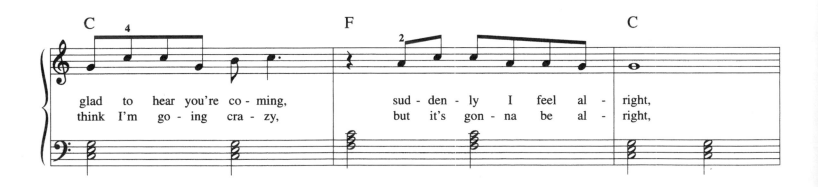

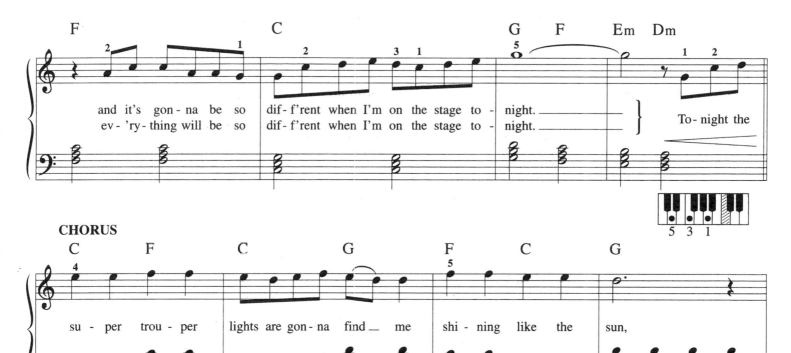

and it's gon-na be so dif-f'rent when I'm on the stage to - night. _____ To- night the

ev-'ry-thing will be so dif-f'rent when I'm on the stage to - night. _____

CHORUS

su - per trou - per lights are gon - na find __ me shi - ning like the sun,

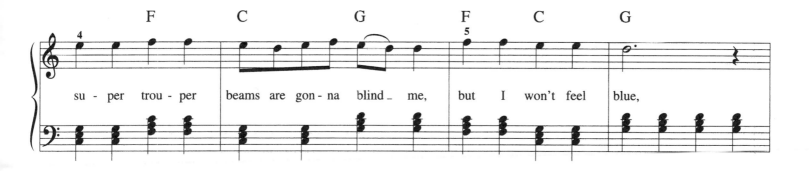

smi - ling, ha - ving fun, feel - ing like a num - ber one. To night the

su - per trou - per beams are gon - na blind __ me, but I won't feel blue,

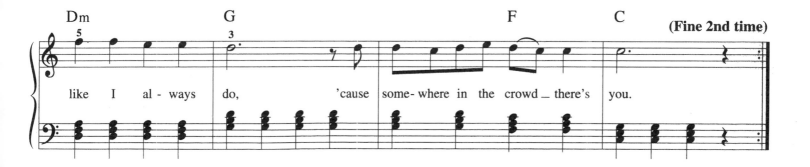

(Fine 2nd time)

like I al - ways do, 'cause some - where in the crowd __ there's you.

Scarborough Fair / Canticle

Arrangements & Original Counter Melody by Paul Simon & Art Garfunkel

2. She's to make me a cam - - - bric

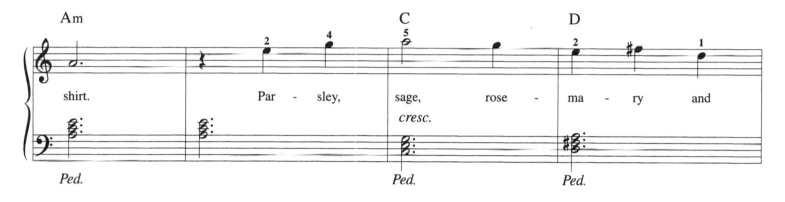

shirt. Par - sley, sage, rose - ma - ry and

cresc.

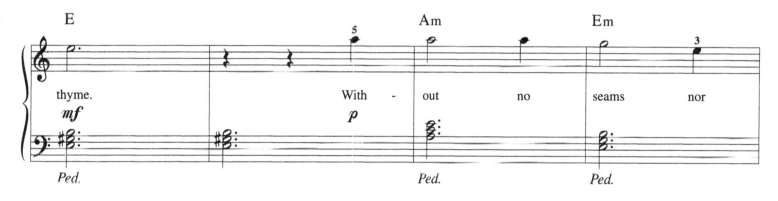

thyme. With - out no seams nor

mf *p*

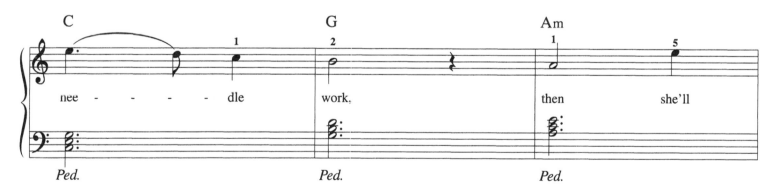

nee - - - - dle work, then she'll

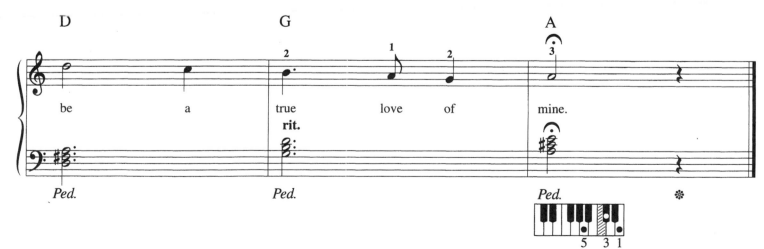

be a true love of mine.

rit.

5 3 1

Sailing

Words & Music by Gavin Sutherland

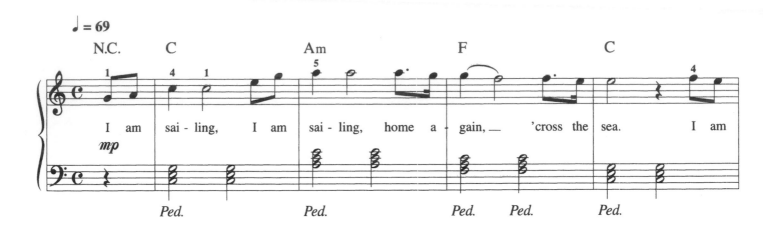

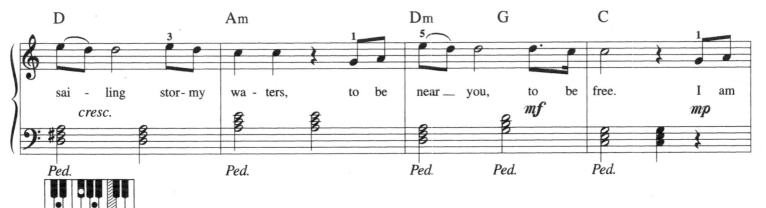

The Lady In Red

Words & Music by Chris de Burgh

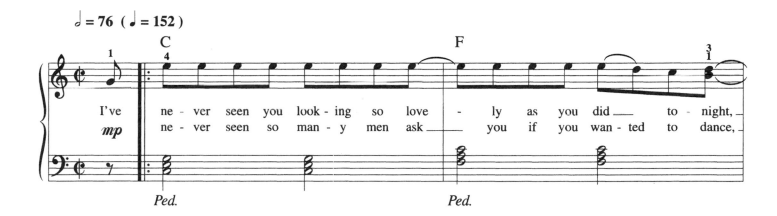

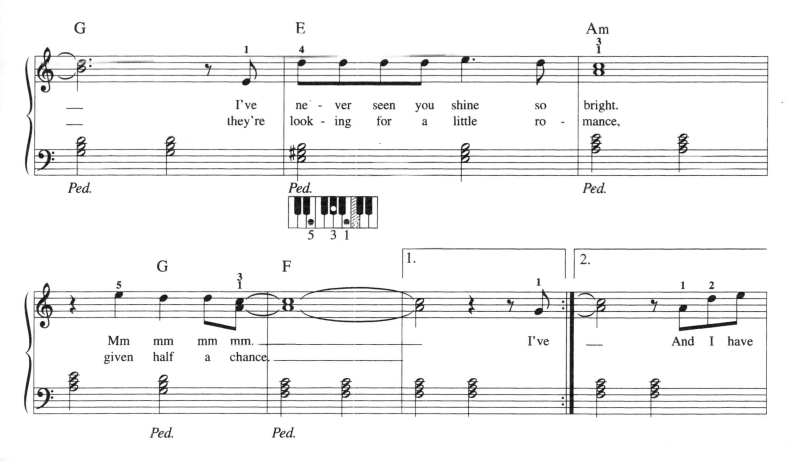

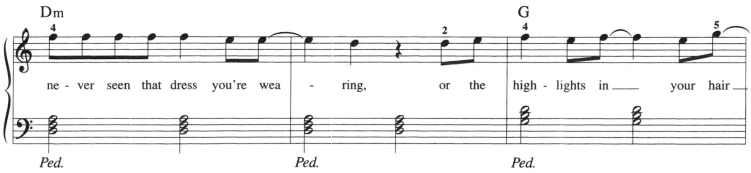

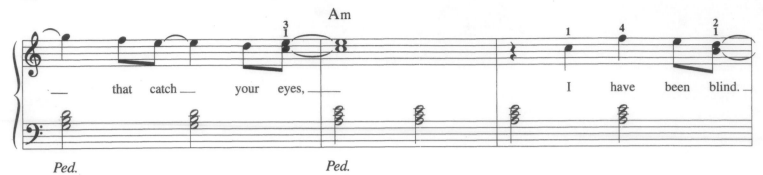

that catch your eyes, I have been blind.

CHORUS

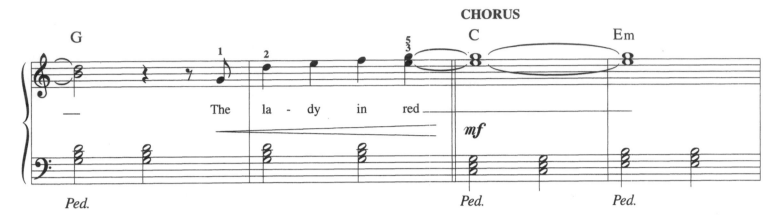

The la - dy in red

mf

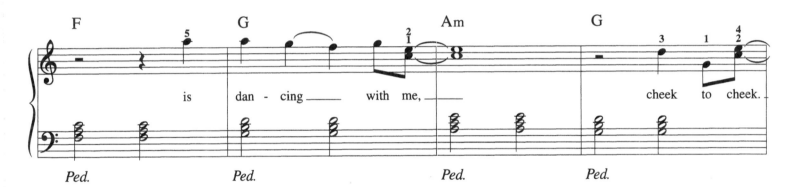

is dan - cing with me, cheek to cheek.

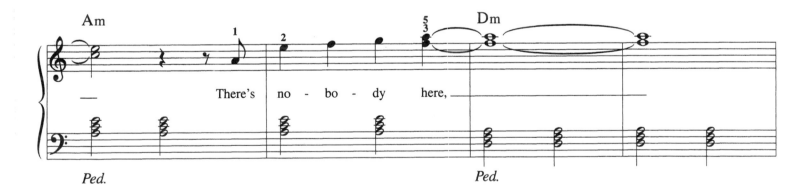

There's no - bo - dy here,

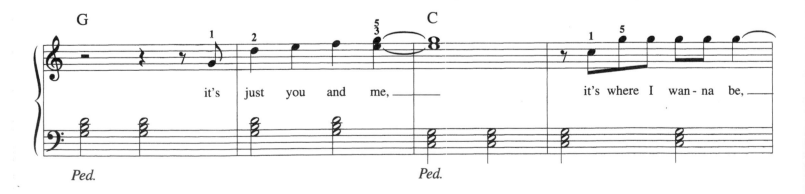

it's just you and me, it's where I wan - na be,

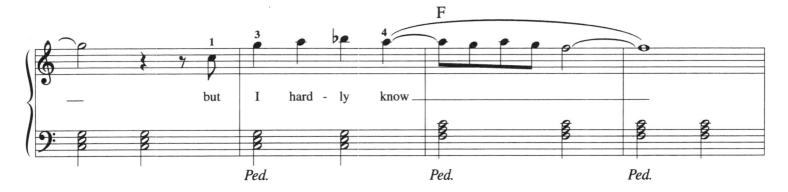

but I hard - ly know ___

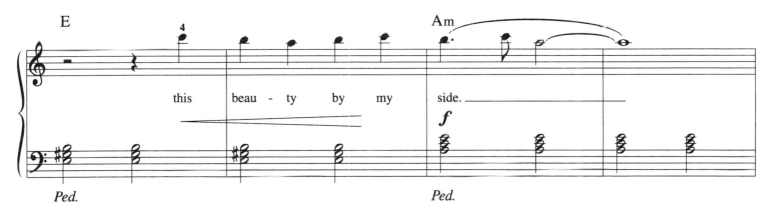

this beau - ty by my side. ___

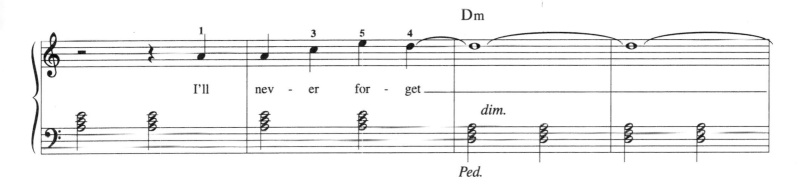

I'll nev - er for - get ___

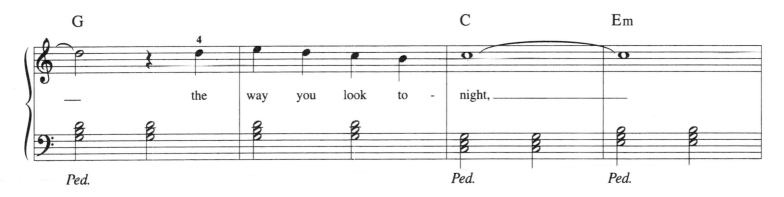

the way you look to - night, ___

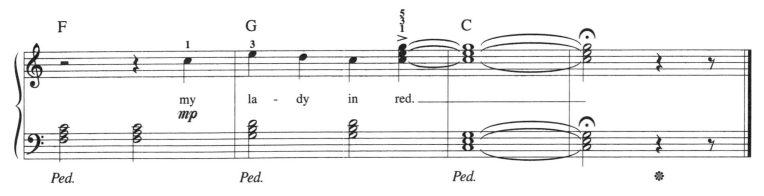

my la - dy in red. ___

Up to now you have been playing in the key of **C major**, which requires no sharps or flats. The next few pieces are written in the key of **F major**. This key is derived from the scale of F (major) which requires one flat: B♭ -

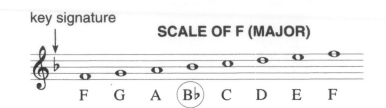

key signature

SCALE OF F (MAJOR)

F G A (B♭) C D E F

You must remember to play every B - **wherever it occurs on the keyboard** - as **B flat**.

New chords:

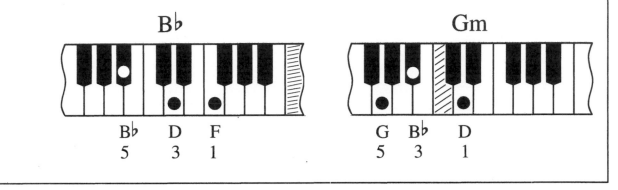

Guantanamera

Words by Jose Marti.
Music Adaptation by Hector Angulo and Pete Seeger

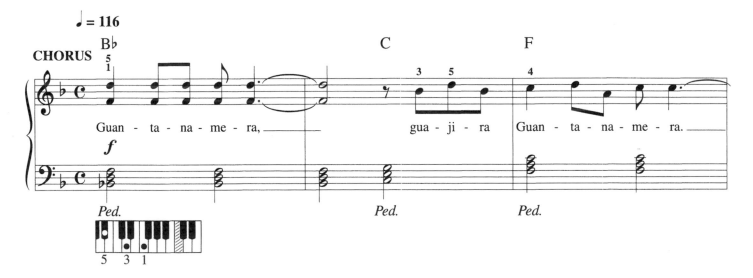

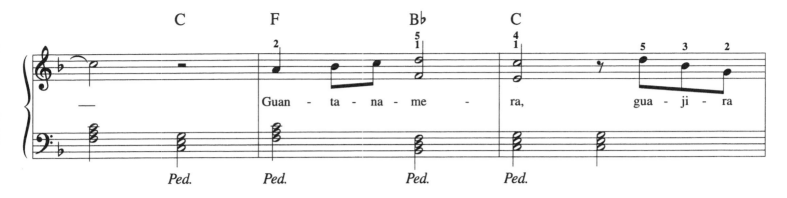

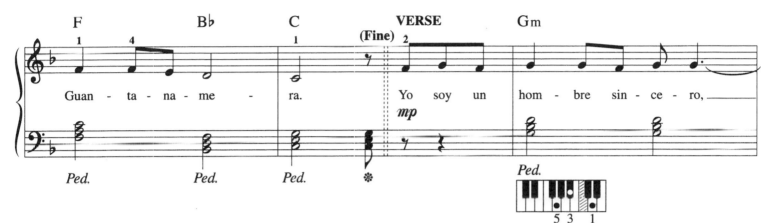

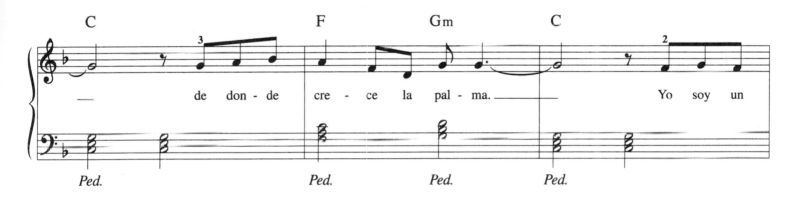

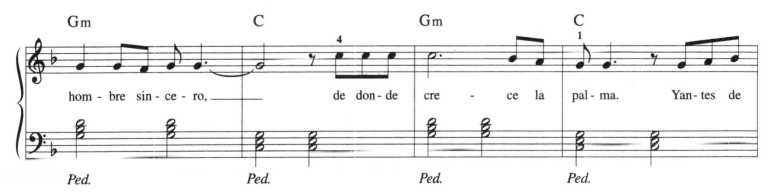

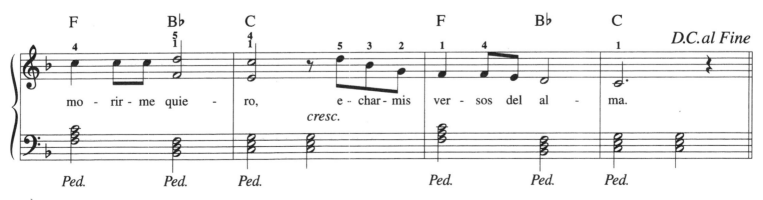

There Goes My Everything

Words & Music by Dallas Frazier

CHORUS

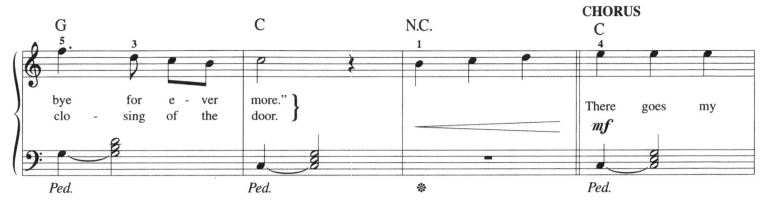

bye   for   e - ver   more."
clo - sing   of the   door. }

There   goes   my

mf

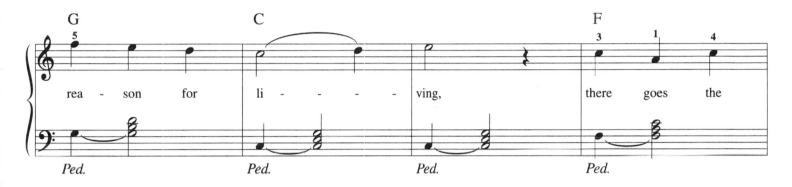

rea - son   for   li - - - - ving,

there   goes   the

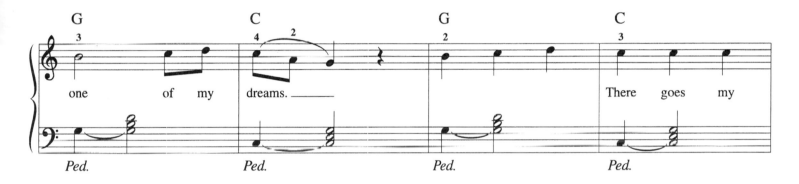

one   of   my   dreams. _____

There   goes   my

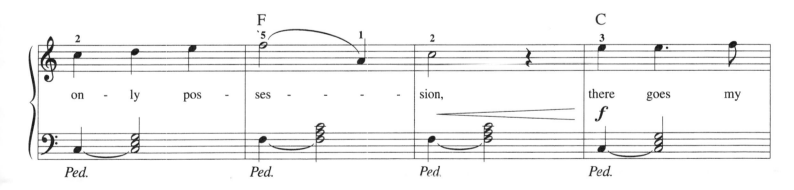

on - ly   pos - ses - - - - - sion,

there   goes   my

f

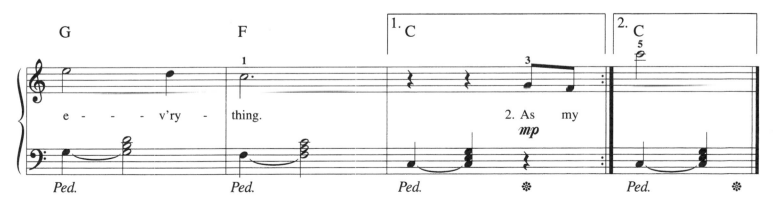

e - - - v'ry - thing.

1.

2. As   my
mp

Anniversary Song

Words & Music by Al Jolson & Saul Chaplin

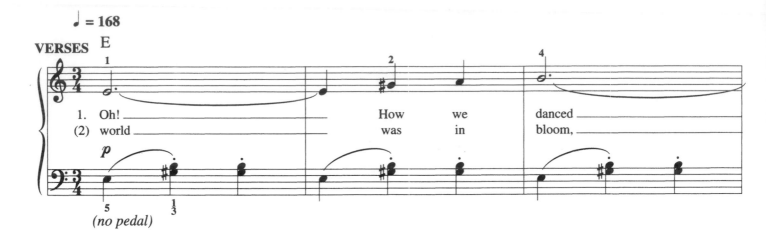

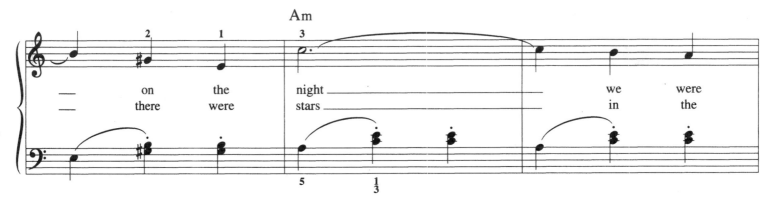

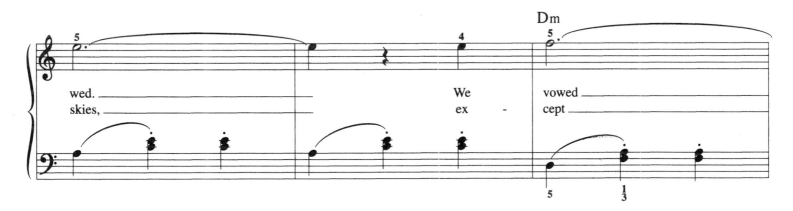

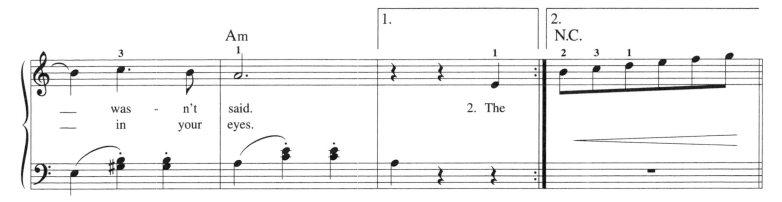

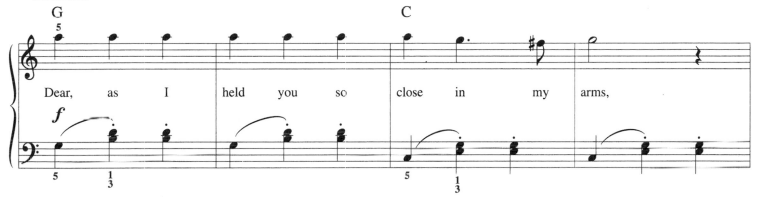

CHORUS

Dear, as I held you so close in my arms,

an - gels were sing - ing a hymn to your charms. Two

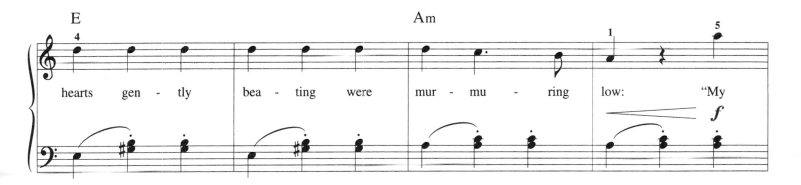

hearts gen - tly bea - ting were mur - mu - ring low: "My

dar - ling, I love you so."

CHORD PYRAMIDS

In this attractive accompaniment style, each note of the triad is played separately, then held down to form a sort of musical pyramid:

GREEN GREEN GRASS OF HOME

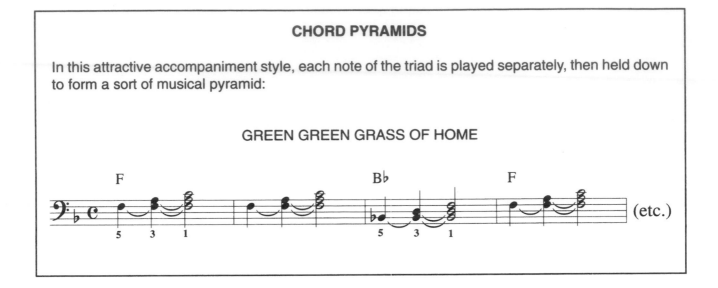

Green Green Grass Of Home

Words & Music by Curly Putman

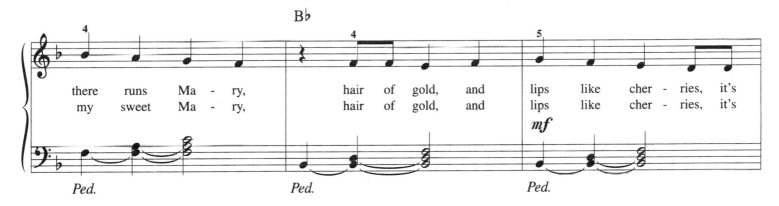

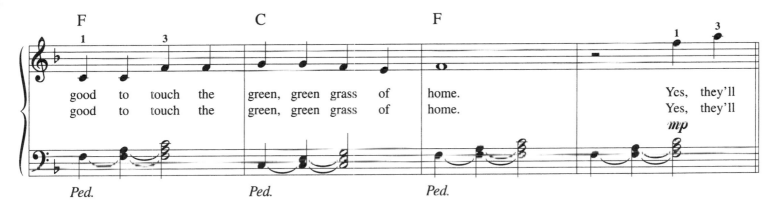

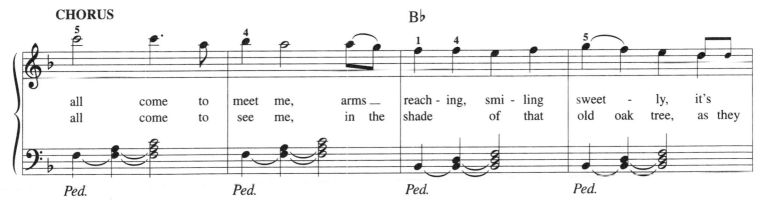

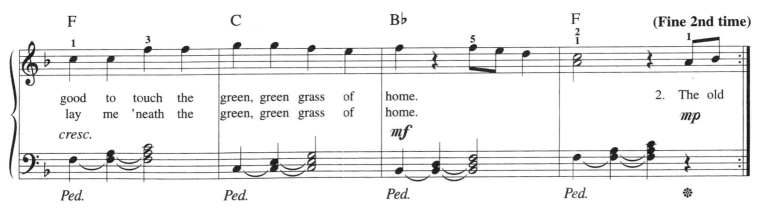

One Moment In Time

Words & Music by Albert Hammond & John Bettis

Imagine

Words & Music by John Lennon

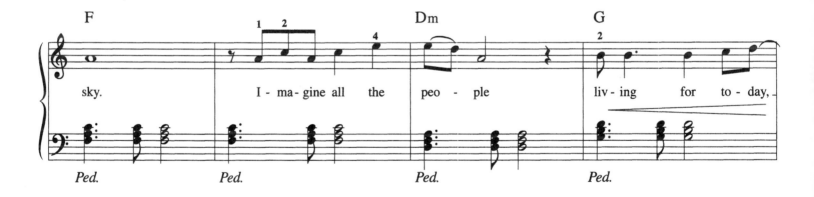

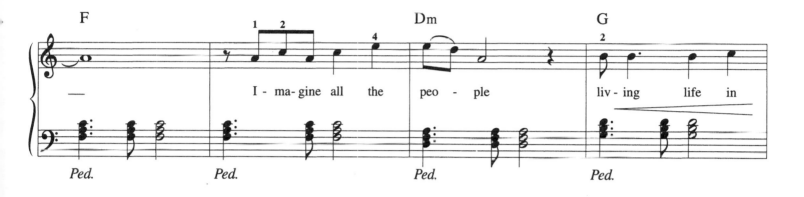

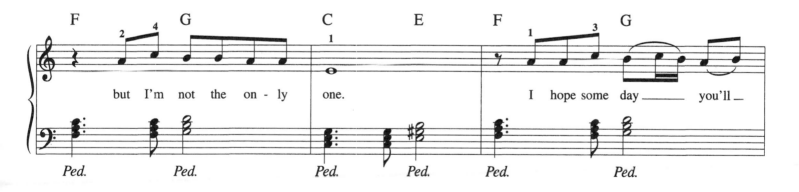

By The Time I Get To Phoenix

Words & Music by Jim Webb

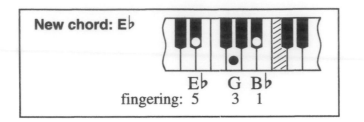

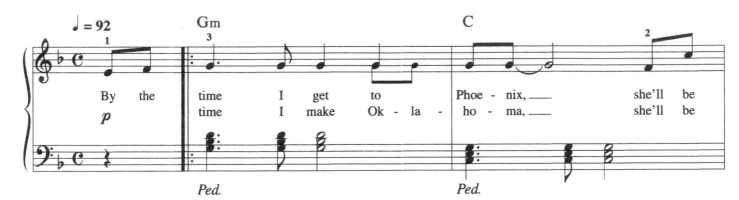

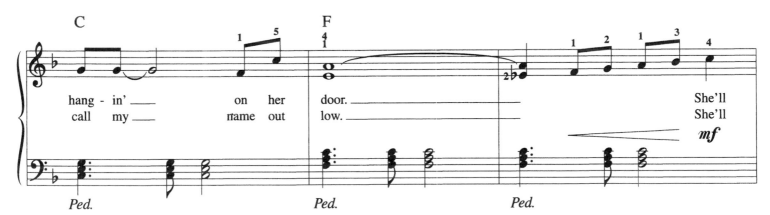

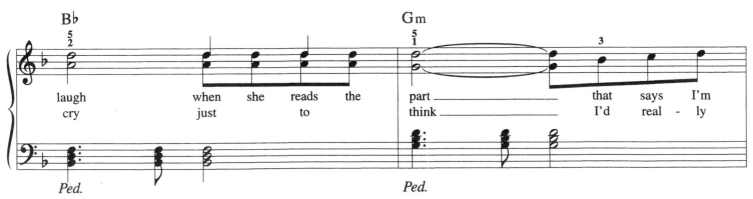

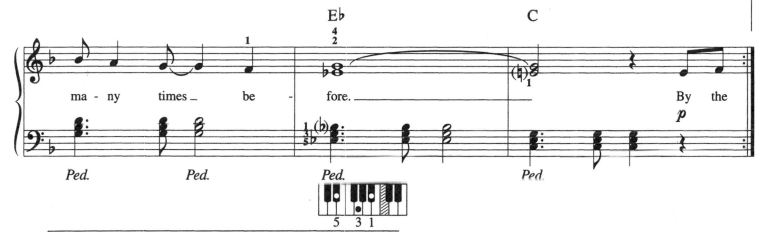

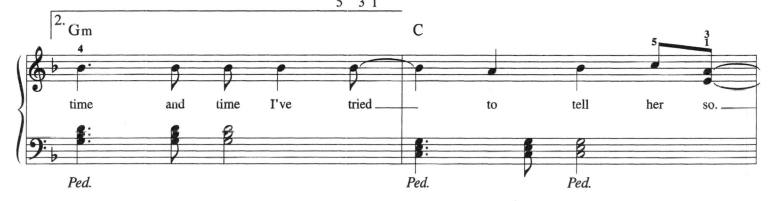

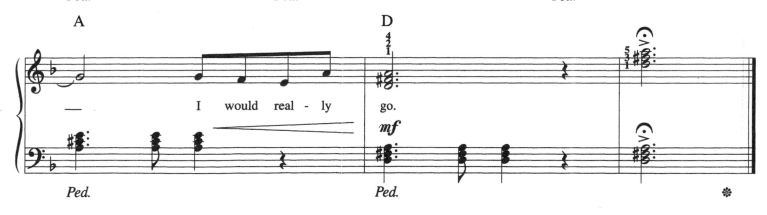

(Everything I Do) I Do It For You

Words by Bryan Adams & Robert John 'Mutt' Lange. Music by Michael Kamen

Your Cheatin' Heart

Words & Music by Hank Williams

> The top note of every triad is called the 5th (because it is **five** letter names up from its bottom note, or root).
>
> To create the following **boogie style** accompaniments, the top note (5th) of each triad moves up a note to the 6th, and back again to the 5th.
>
> To keep things simple, 6ths have not been included in the chord symbols.

will tell on you. When tears come down, *mp*

like fall - in' rain, you'll toss a - round,

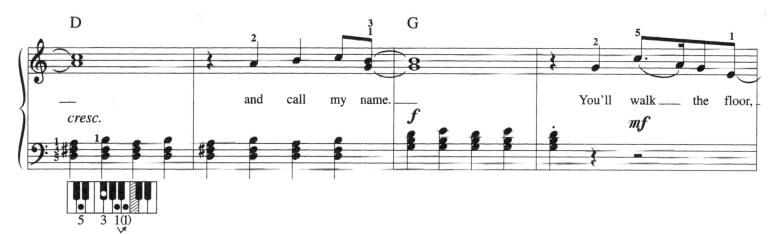

cresc. and call my name. *f* You'll walk the floor, *mf*

the way I do, your chea - tin' heart

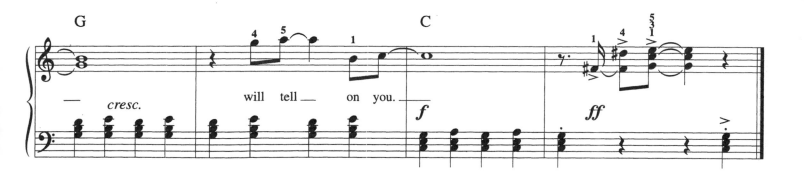

cresc. will tell on you. *f* *ff*

Ob-La-Di, Ob-La-Da

Words & Music by John Lennon & Paul McCartney

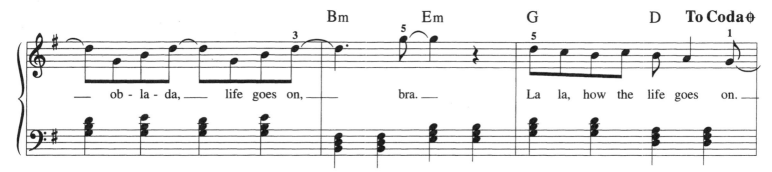

ob - la - da, ___ life goes on, ___ bra. __ La la, how the life goes on. __

In a couple of years they have built a home, __ sweet home.

A couple of kids run - ning

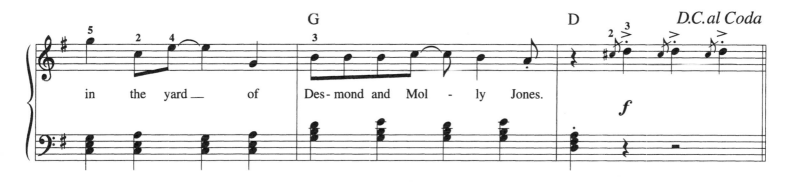

in the yard __ of Des - mond and Mol - ly Jones.

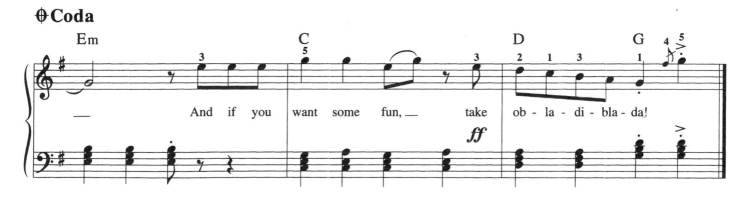

And if you want some fun, __ take ob - la - di - bla - da!

Rock Around The Clock

Words & Music by Max C. Freedman & Jimmy de Knight

rock, rock, rock, 'til broad day-light, we're gon-na rock gon-na rock a-

round the clock __ to-night. _____ When the clock strikes two,

three, and four, if the band slows down we'll yell for more! We're gon-na rock a-round the

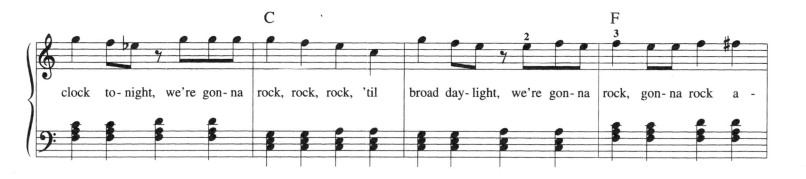

clock to-night, we're gon-na rock, rock, rock, 'til broad day-light, we're gon-na rock, gon-na rock a-

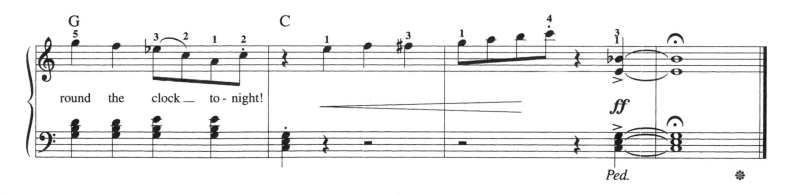

round the clock __ to-night!

ff

Ped. ✲

LOW TRIADS

When triads are played low on the piano they sound 'muddy', and rather ugly.
The simple solution is to OMIT THE MIDDLE NOTE OF THE TRIAD:

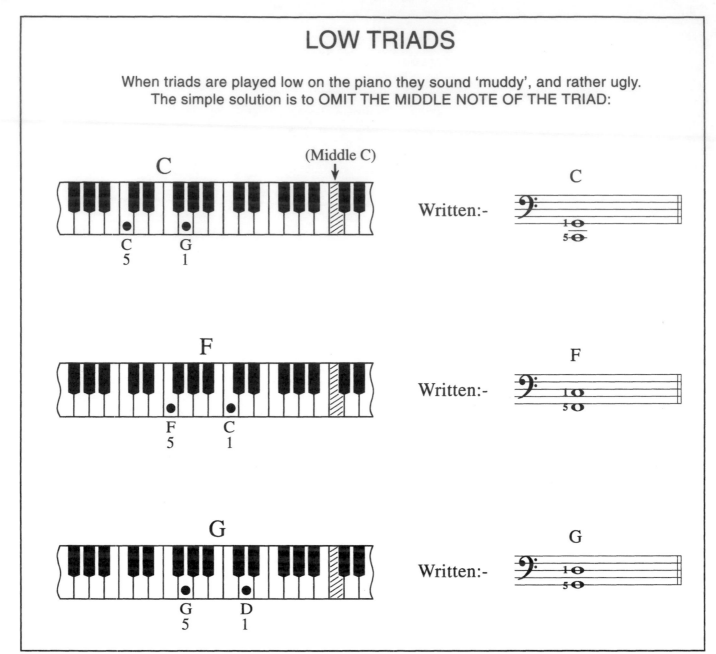

Mull Of Kintyre

Words & Music by McCartney & Laine

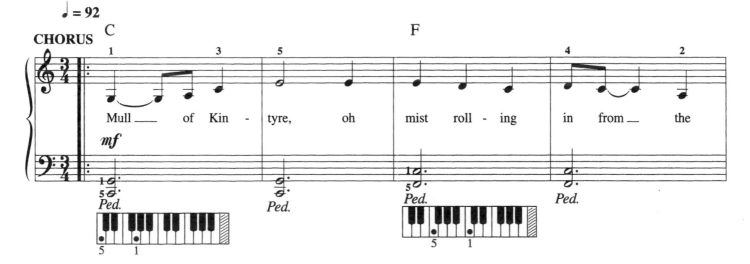

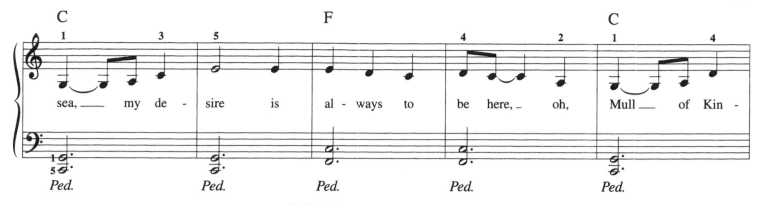

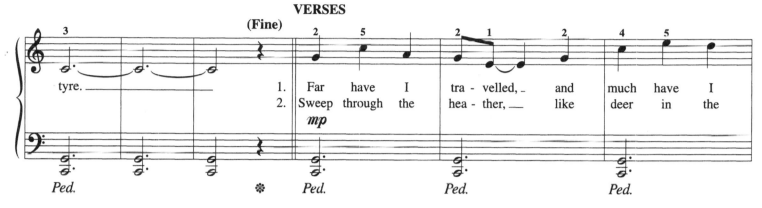

VERSES

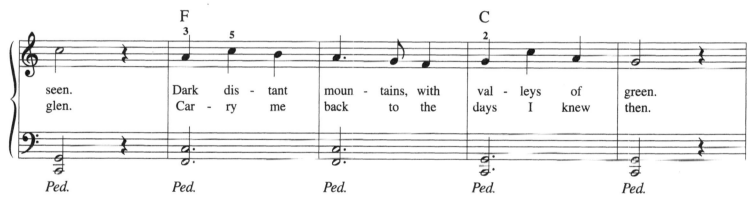

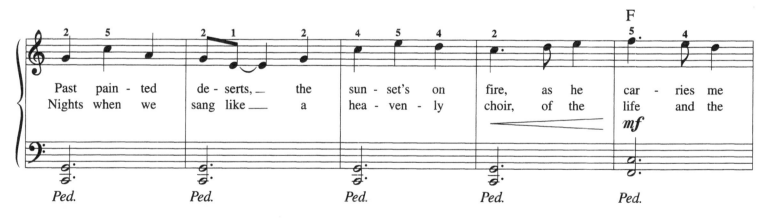

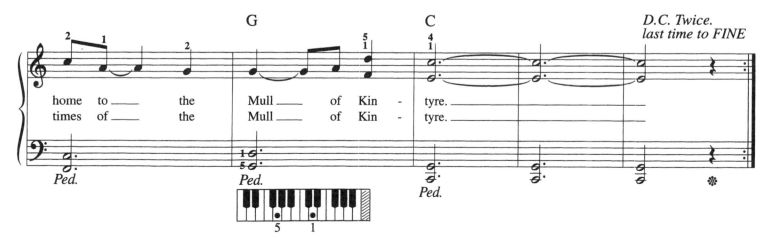

Every Breath You Take

Words & Music by Sting

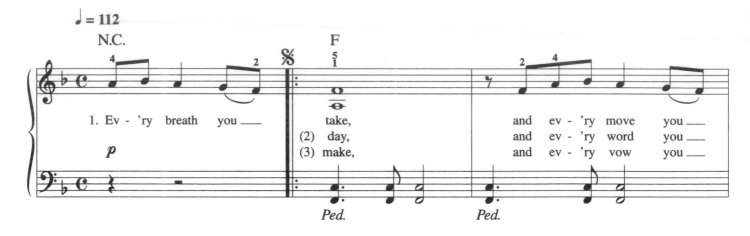

that you be - long to me? My — poor heart —

cresc.

aches _____ with ev - 'ry step you take. _____

f

◊ Coda

D.S. al Coda

3. Ev - 'ry move you —

p

Dm

Ev - 'ry move you make,

mp

B♭ · · · C · · · Dm · · · C

— ev - 'ry step you take, _____ I'll be watch - ing you. _____

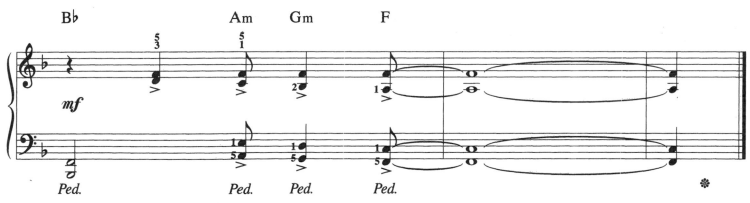

B♭ · · · Am · Gm · · · F

mf

Mamma Mia

Words & Music by Benny Andersson,
Stig Anderson & Bjorn Ulvaeus

In the next two pieces the two low triad notes are played **separately.**

CHORUS

Oh, _____ Mam - ma Mi - a! Here I go _____ a - gain, my, my!

How can I re - sist you? Mam - ma Mi - a! Does it show _____ a - gain,

my, my! Just how much I've missed you, Yes, _____ I've been bro -

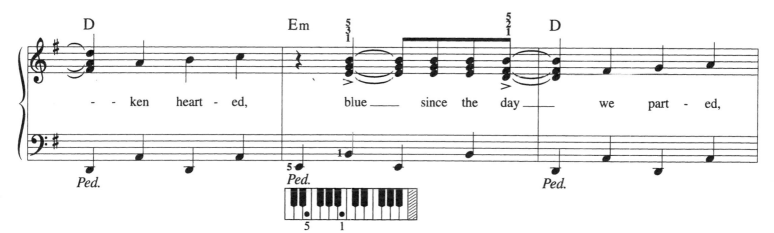

- - ken heart - ed, blue _____ since the day _____ we part - ed,

why, why, did I e - ver let _____ you go? _____ _ff_

The Entertainer

By Scott Joplin

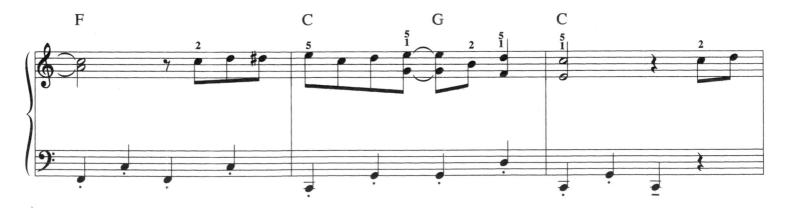

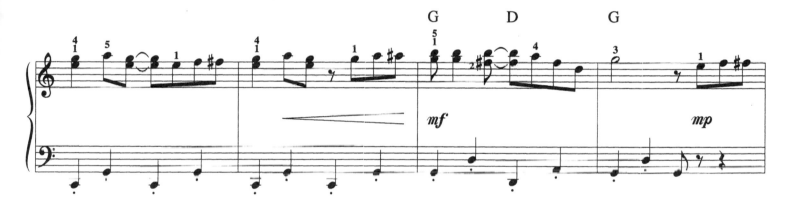

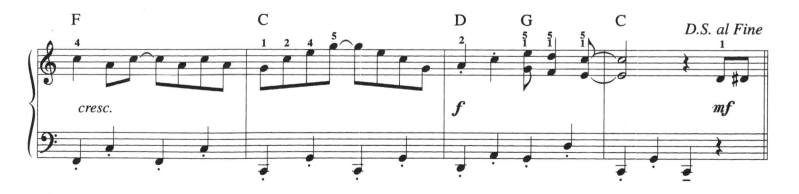

Let It Be

Words & Music by John Lennon & Paul McCartney

> **Seventh chords** are a combination of 'triads' (major or minor), and 7th notes (from major or minor scales). When playing seventh chords the 5th of the triad is usually omitted.

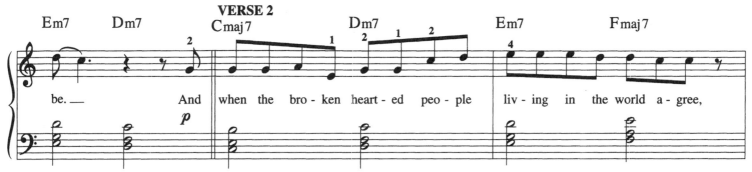

Em7 Dm7 **VERSE 2** Cmaj7 Dm7 Em7 Fmaj7

be. ___ And when the bro - ken heart - ed peo - ple liv - ing in the world a - gree,

p

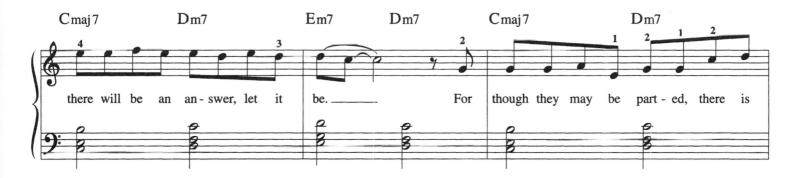

Cmaj7 Dm7 Em7 Dm7 Cmaj7 Dm7

there will be an an - swer, let it be. ___ For though they may be part - ed, there is

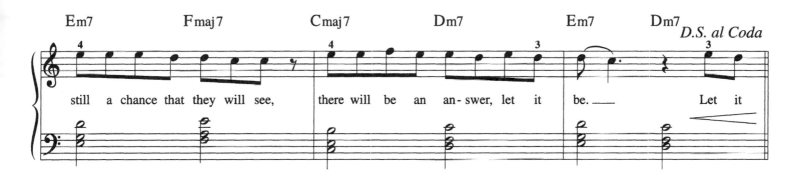

Em7 Fmaj7 Cmaj7 Dm7 Em7 Dm7 *D.S. al Coda*

still a chance that they will see, there will be an an - swer, let it be. ___ Let it

⊕ Coda

Em7 Fmaj7 Em7 Dm7 Cmaj7

be. ___

mf

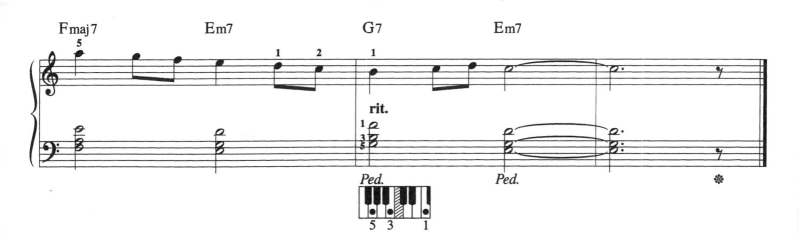

Fmaj7 Em7 G7 Em7

rit.

Ped. *Ped.*

5 3 1

The Fifty-Ninth Street Bridge Song
(Feelin' Groovy)

Words & Music by Paul Simon

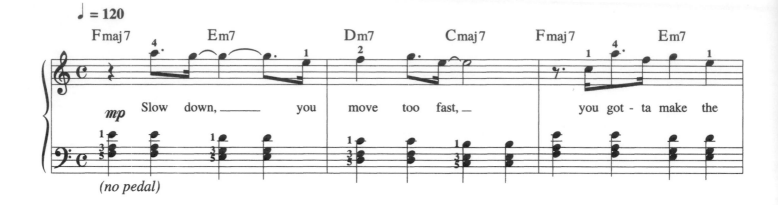

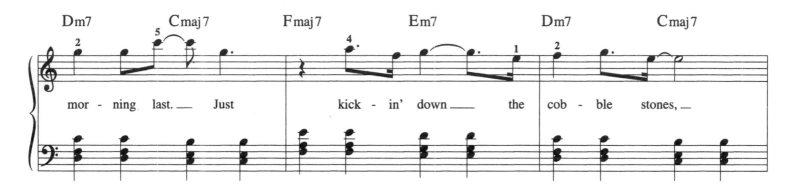

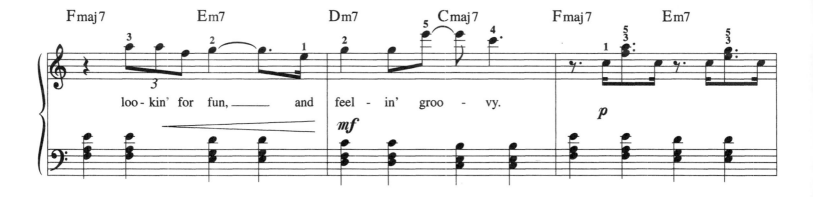

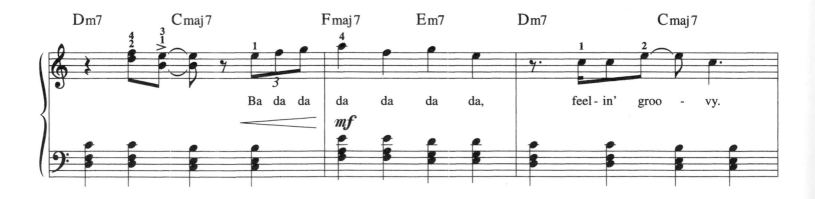

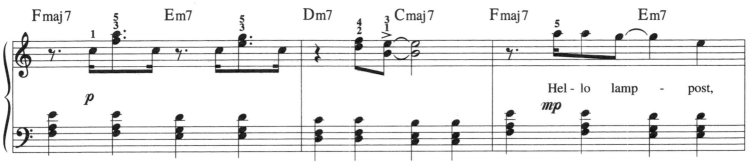

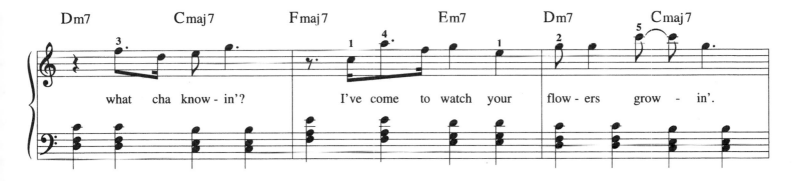

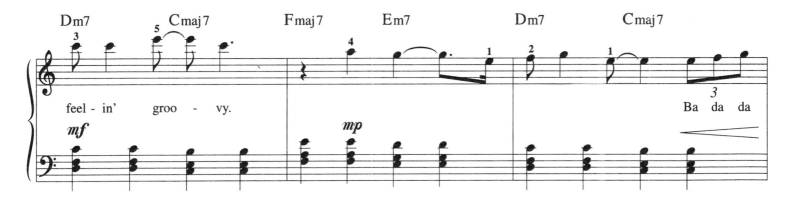

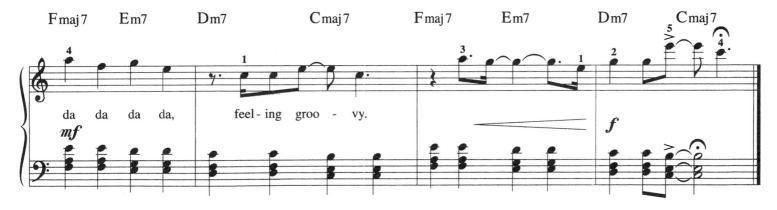

All I Ask Of You

Music by Andrew Lloyd Webber. Lyrics by Charles Hart.
Additional lyrics by Richard Stilgoe

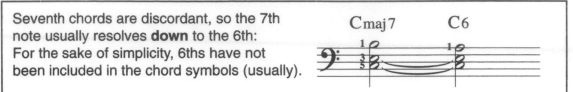

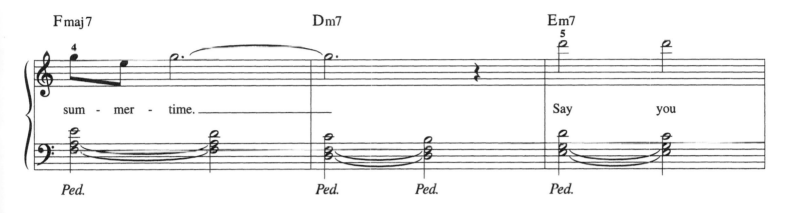

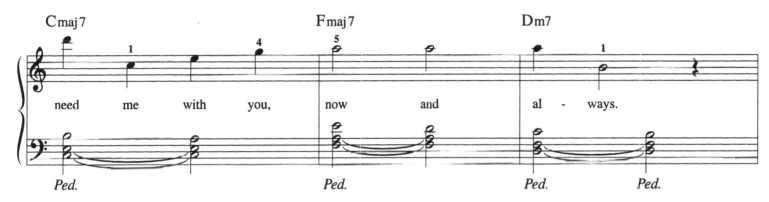

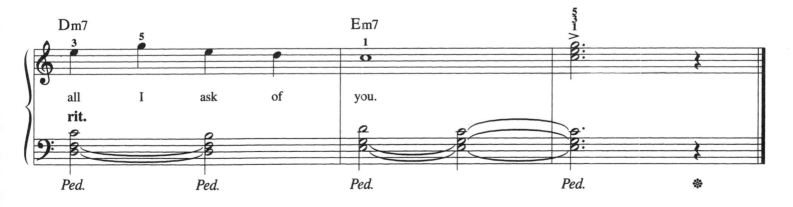

Falling In Love Again

Music & Original Words by Friedrich Hollander.
English Words by Reg Connelly

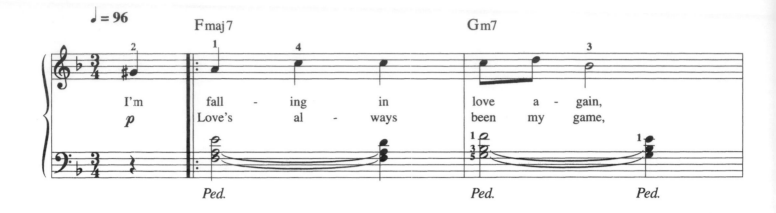

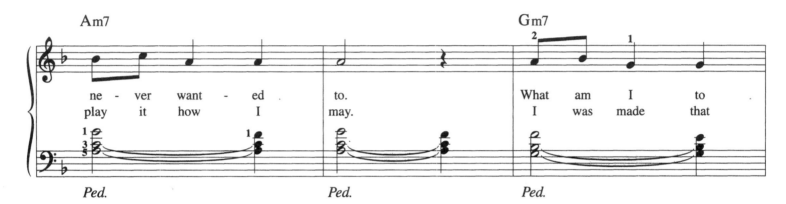

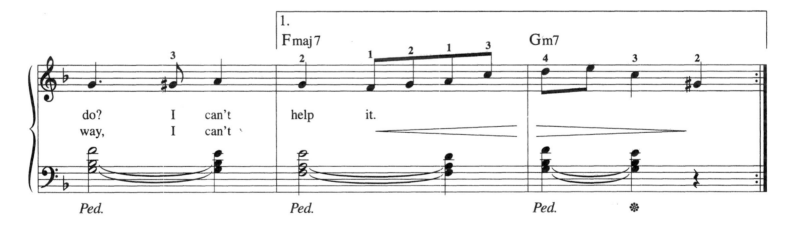

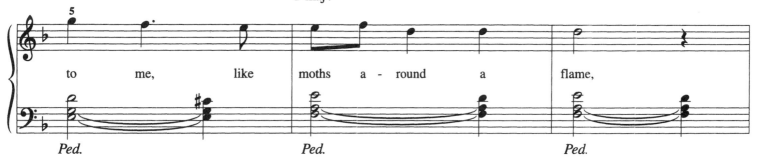

to me,   like   moths a - round   a   flame,

and   if   their   wings   burn,   I   know   I'm   not   to

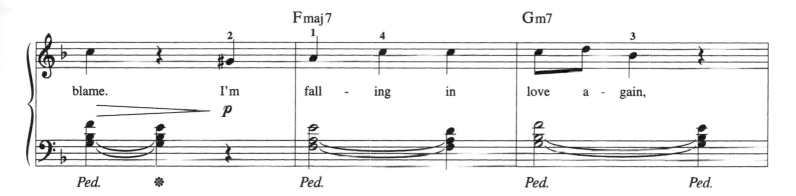

blame.   I'm   fall - ing   in   love   a - gain,

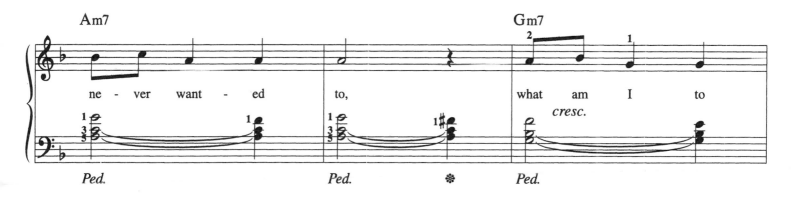

ne - ver   want - ed   to,   what   am   I   to

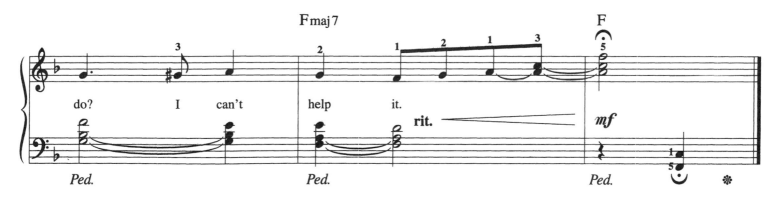

do?   I   can't   help   it.

Have I Told You Lately

Words & Music by Van Morrison

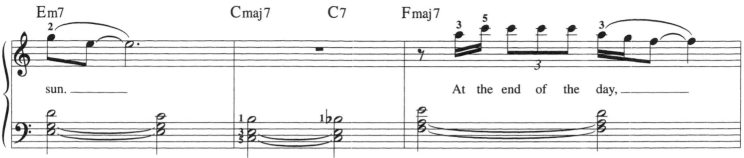

sun. _____

At the end of the day, _____

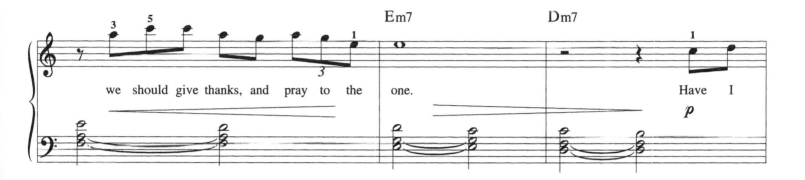

we should give thanks, and pray to the one.

Have I

told you late-ly that I love _ you,

have I told you there's no-one _ a-

bove _ you?

Fill my heart with glad-ness,

take a-way my sad-ness,

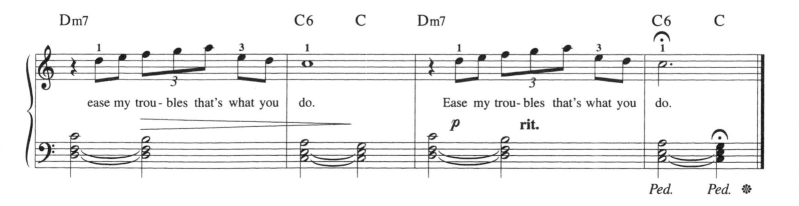

ease my trou-bles that's what you do.

Ease my trou-bles that's what you do.

Ped.   Ped. ✲

Copacabana (At The Copa)

Words & Music by Barry Manilow, Bruce Sussman & Jack Feldman

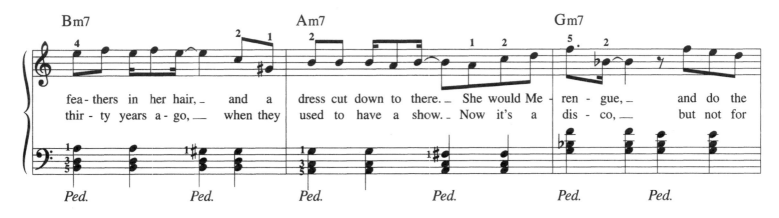

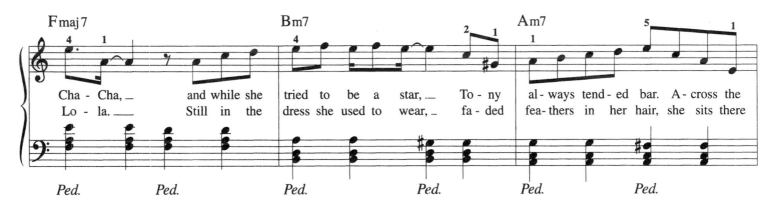

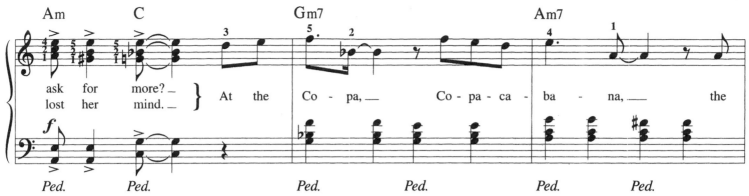

ask for more? —
lost her mind. —
} At the Co - pa, — Co - pa - ca - ba - na, — the

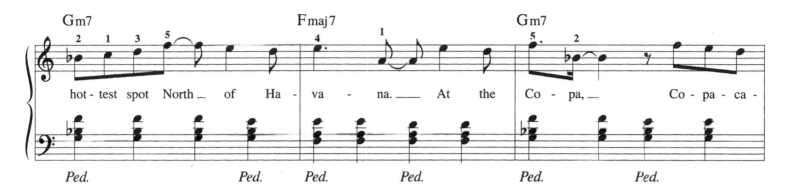

hot - test spot North — of Ha - va - na. — At the Co - pa, — Co - pa - ca -

ba - na, — mu - sic and pas - sion were al - ways the fa - shion, at the

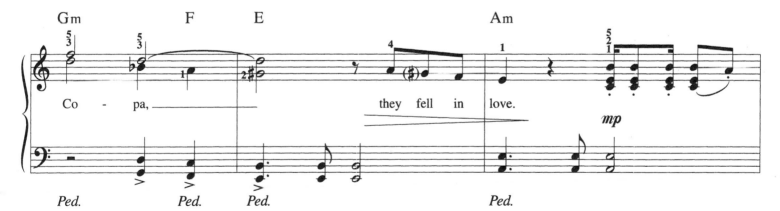

Co - pa, — they fell in love.

(Repeat and fade ad lib.)

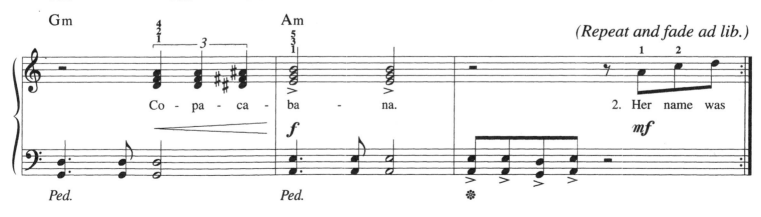

Co - pa - ca - ba - na. 2. Her name was

Just An Old Fashioned Girl

Words & Music by Marve Fisher

67

On This Night Of A Thousand Stars

Words by Tim Rice. Music by Andrew Lloyd Webber

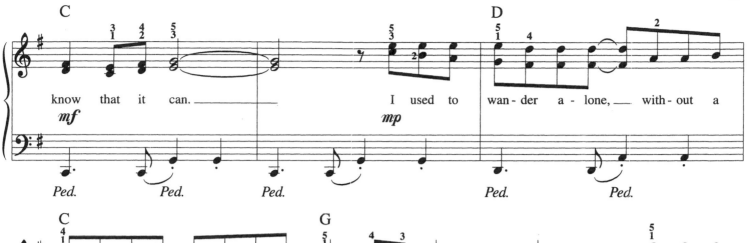

C   D

know that it can. _____   I used to wan - der a - lone, _ with - out a

C   G

love of my own, _ I was a des - per - ate man. _____   But all my

                                                C

grief dis - ap - peared, _ and all the sor - row I'd feared, _ was - n't there an - y - more, _

Cm   G   D

_   on that ma - gi - cal day, _ when you first came my way, _ mi a -

G   1.   D.S.   2.

mor.   On this night of a

Perfidia

English Lyric by Milton Leeds. Music & Spanish Words by Alberto Dominguez

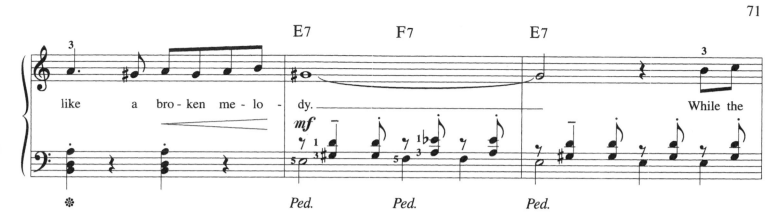

like a bro - ken me - lo - dy. _____ While the

gods of love look down and laugh at what ro - man - tic fools we mor - tals be.

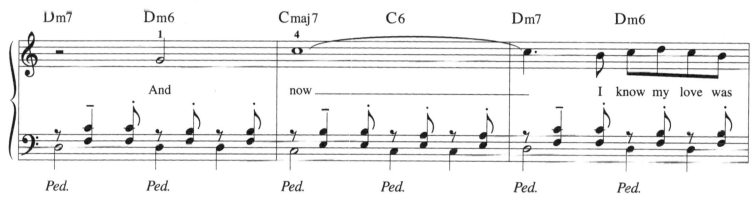

And now _____ I know my love was

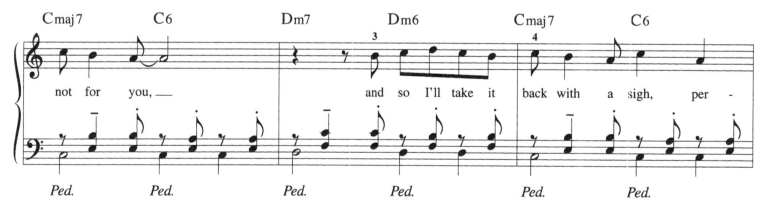

not for you, ___ and so I'll take it back with a sigh, per -

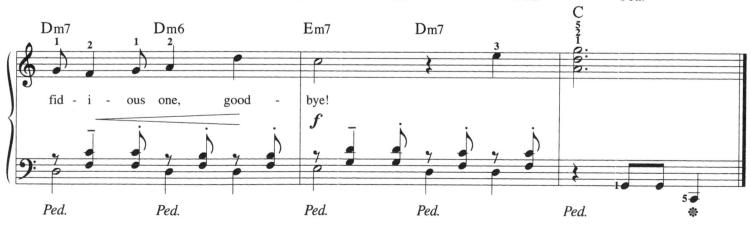

fid - i - ous one, good - bye!

House Of The Rising Sun

Traditional

The key of D minor is derived from the **scale** of D minor, which requires one flat: B♭:-

Scale of D minor (natural form)

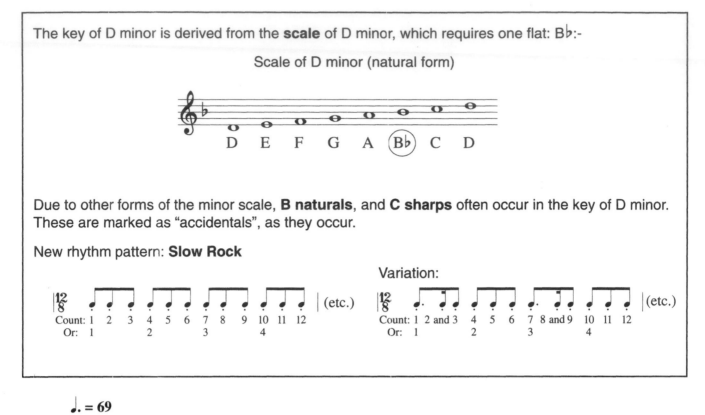

D E F G A (B♭) C D

Due to other forms of the minor scale, **B naturals**, and **C sharps** often occur in the key of D minor. These are marked as "accidentals", as they occur.

New rhythm pattern: **Slow Rock**

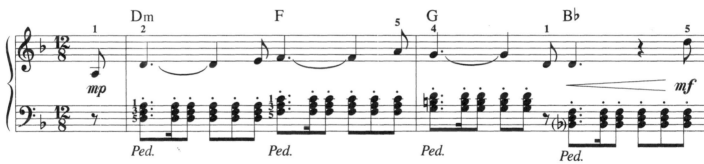

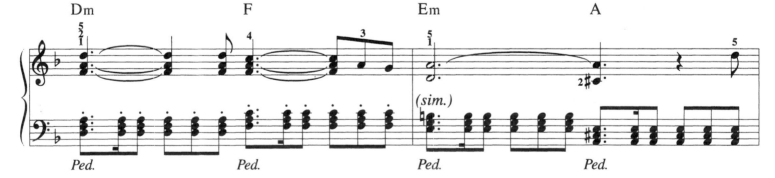

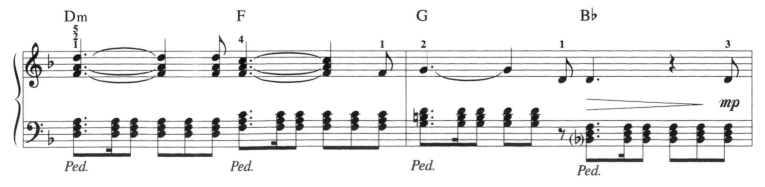

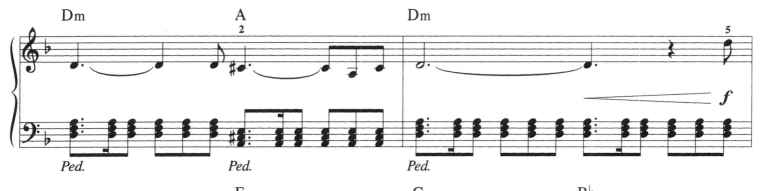

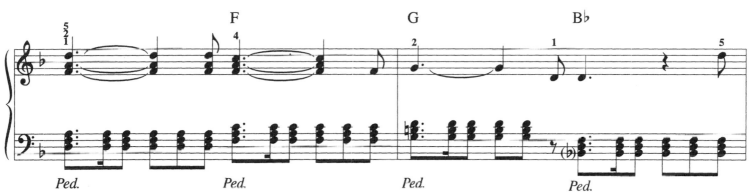

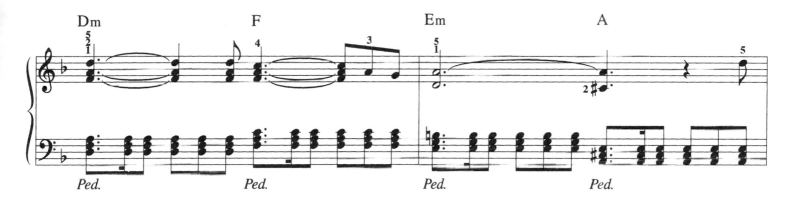

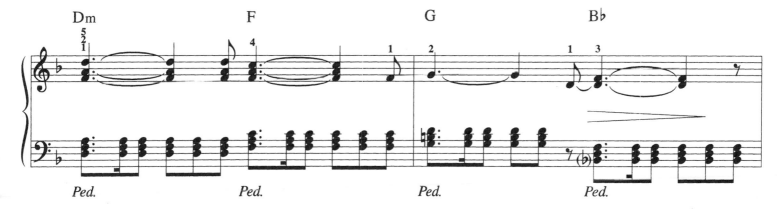

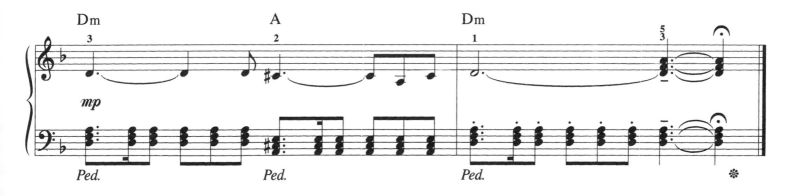

Sunrise Sunset

Words by Sheldon Harnick. Music by Jerry Bock

pass.

Ped. Ped. Ped. Ped.

CHORUS

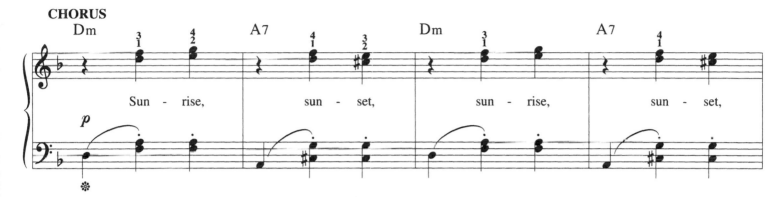

Sun - rise, sun - set, sun - rise, sun - set,

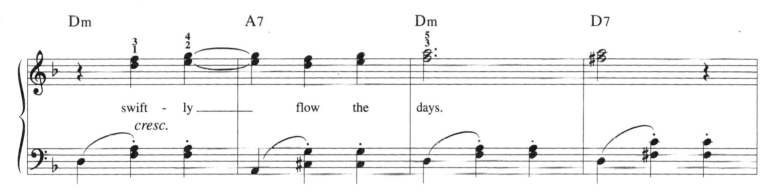

swift - ly _____ flow the days.

cresc.

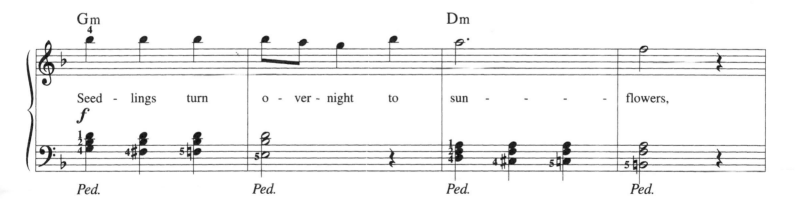

Seed - lings turn o - ver - night to sun - - - - flowers,

Ped. Ped. Ped. Ped.

blos - som - ing e - ven as we gaze. _____

Ped.

Feelings (Dime)

By Morris Albert & Louis Gaste

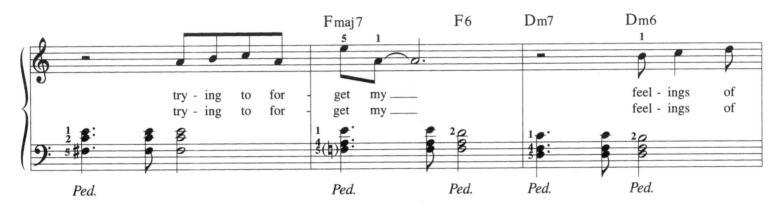

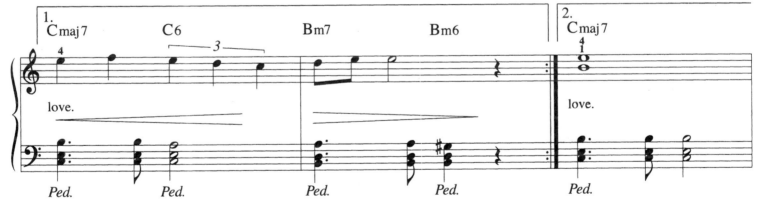

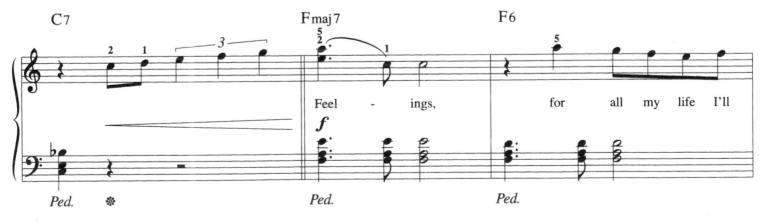

* See p. 16

I Left My Heart In San Francisco

Words by Douglas Cross. Music by George Cory

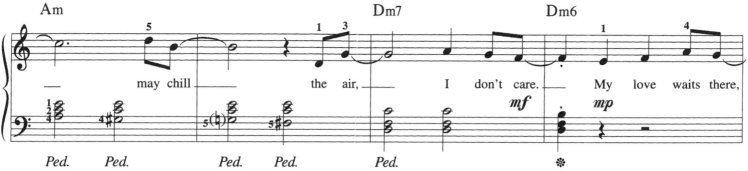

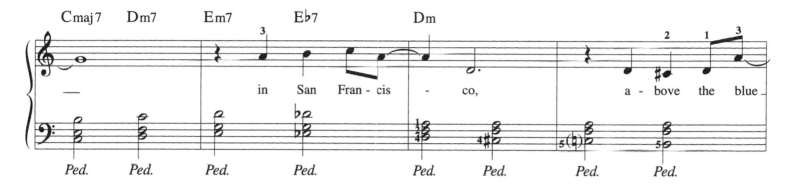

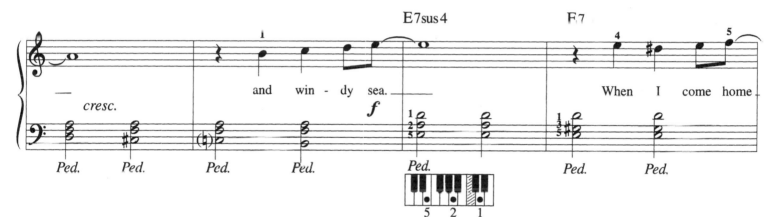

Georgia On My Mind

Words by Stuart Gorrell.
Music by Hoagy Carmichael

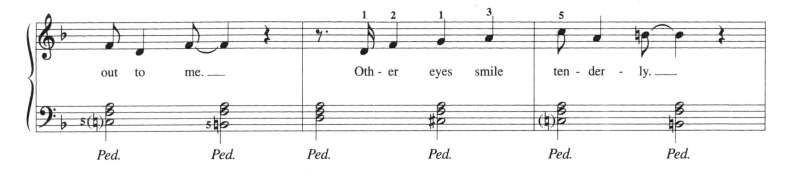

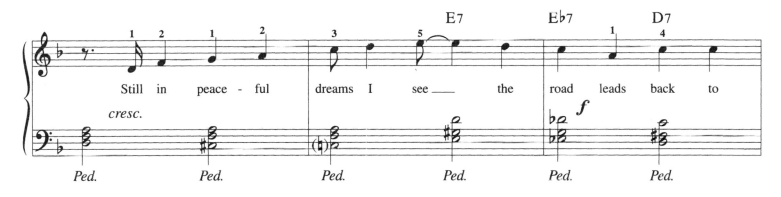

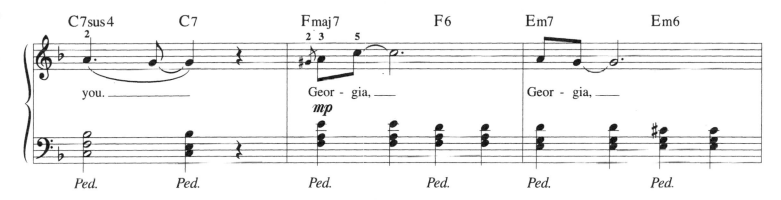

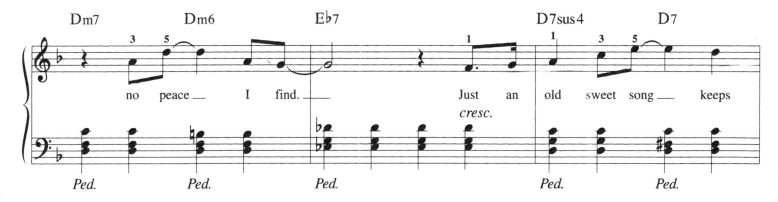

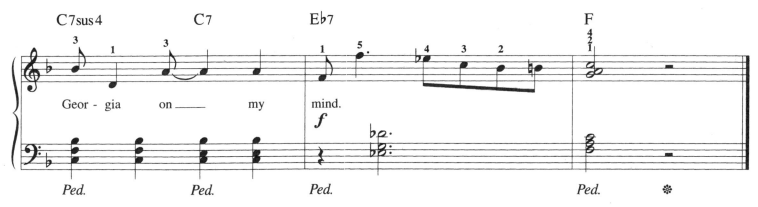

Raindrops Keep Falling On My Head

Words by Hal David. Music by Burt Bacharach

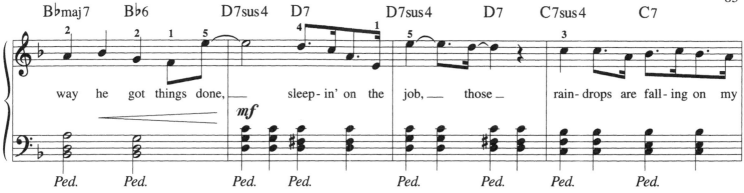

way he got things done,___ sleep-in' on the job,___ those ___ rain-drops are fall-ing on my

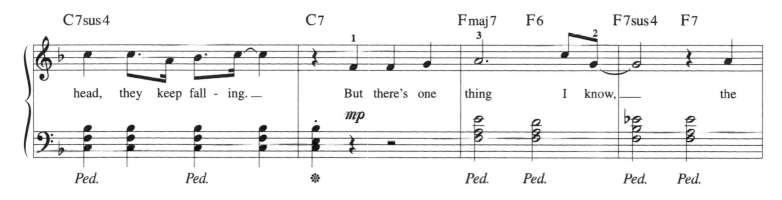

head, they keep fall - ing.___ But there's one thing I know,___ the

blues they send to meet me, won't de - feat me,___ it won't be long, — till

hap - pi - ness steps up to greet me.___

⊕ Coda **Slower**

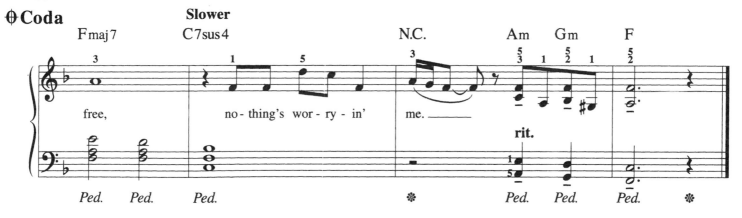

free, no - thing's wor - ry - in' me. ___

Hit The Road Jack

Words & Music by Percy Mayfield

Octaves in the left hand make an effective new type of accompaniment.
New Keys: E♭ major, and C minor. Both keys have the same key signature: though C minor often requires A♮ and B♮ as accidentals.

85

CHORUS

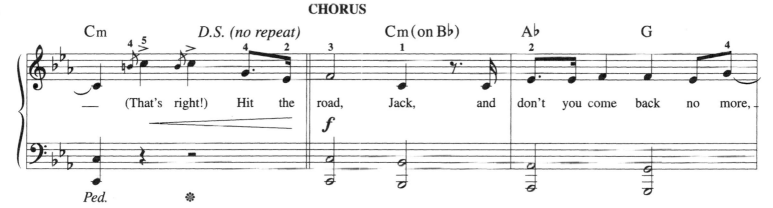

(Repeat and fade)

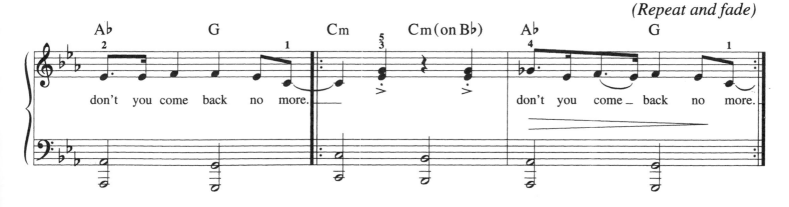

Could It Be Magic

Words & Music by Barry Manilow & Adrienne Anderson

87

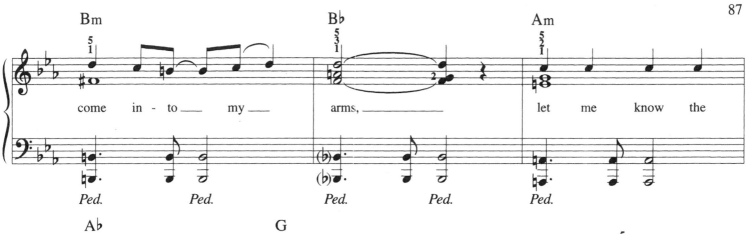

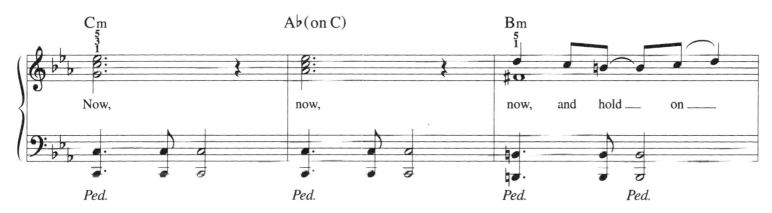

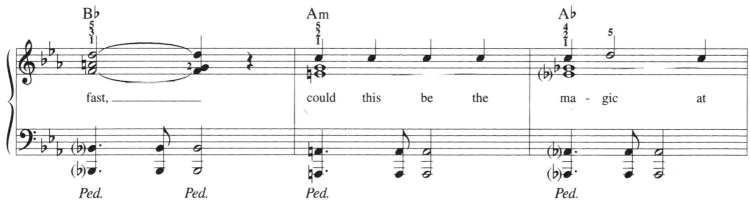

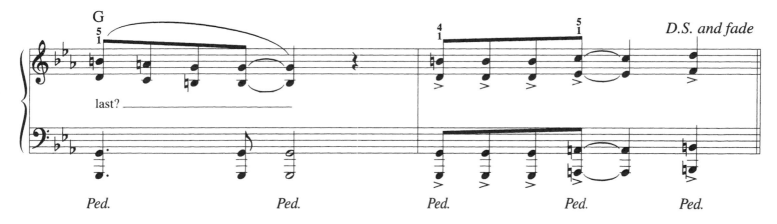

Don't Blame Me

Words & Music by Jimmy McHugh & Dorothy Fields

I Got Rhythm

Music & Lyrics by George Gershwin & Ira Gershwin

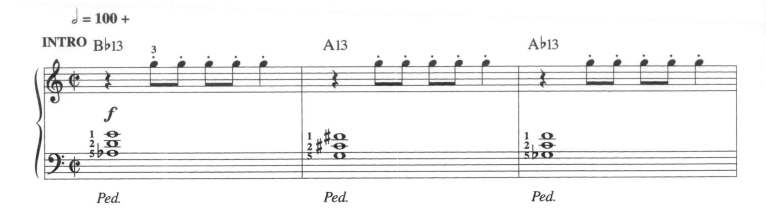

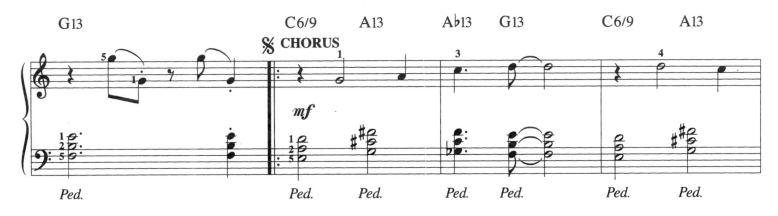

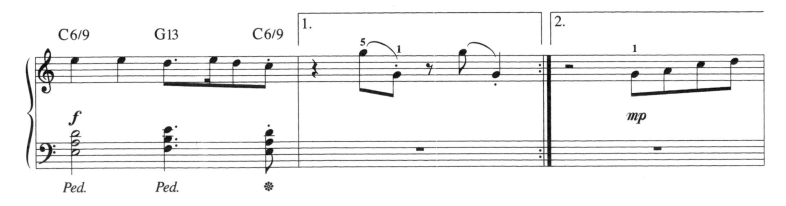

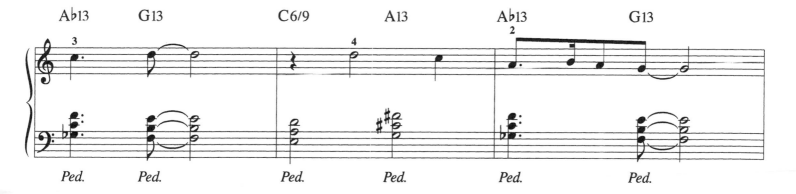

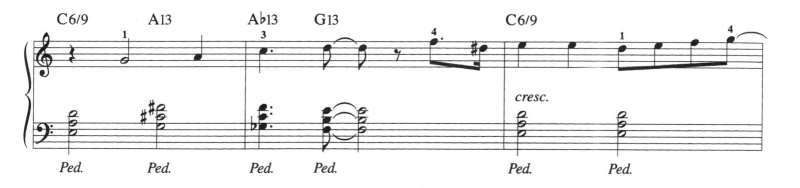

IMPROVISATION

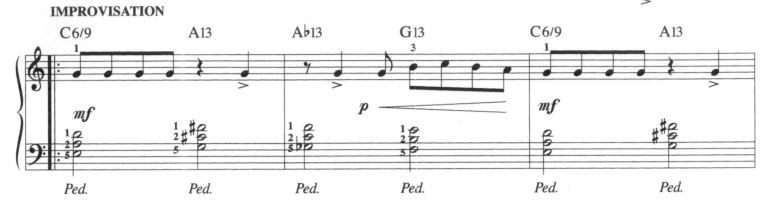

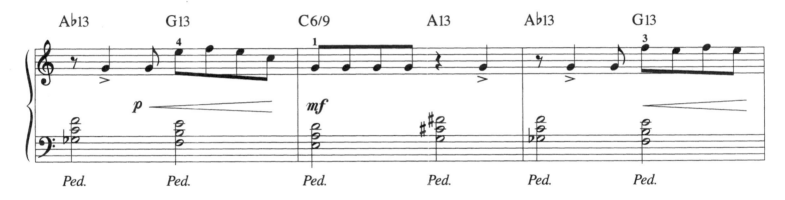

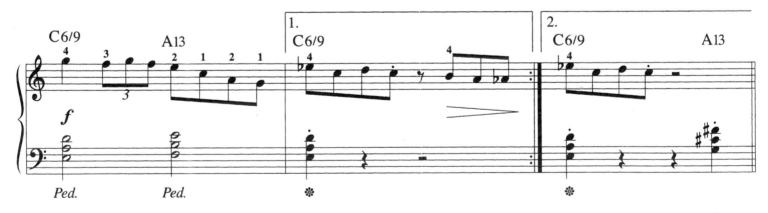

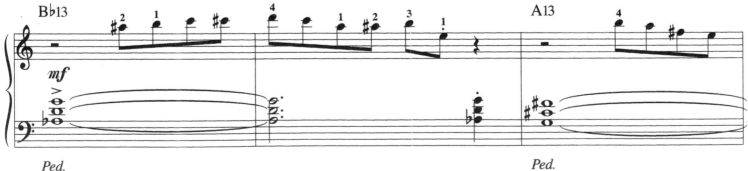

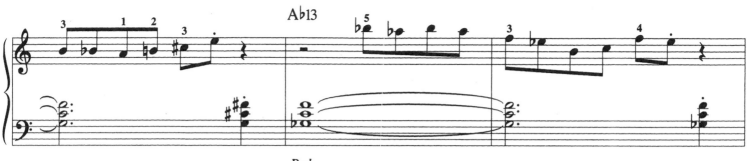

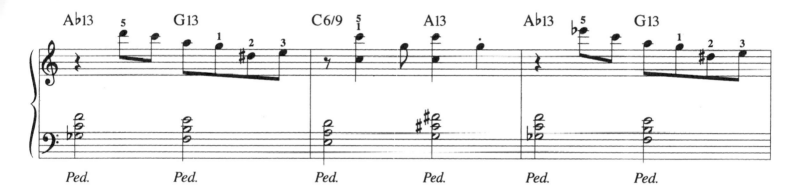

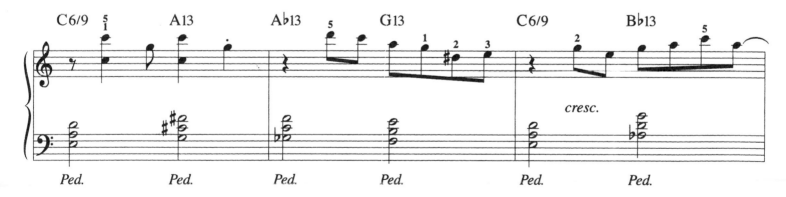

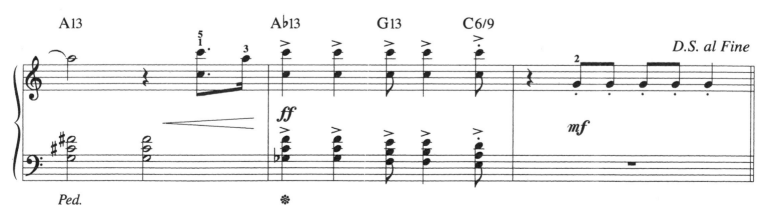

The **chord by chord** symbols in this book are based on **triads**.
This is a three note chord with the following spacing:

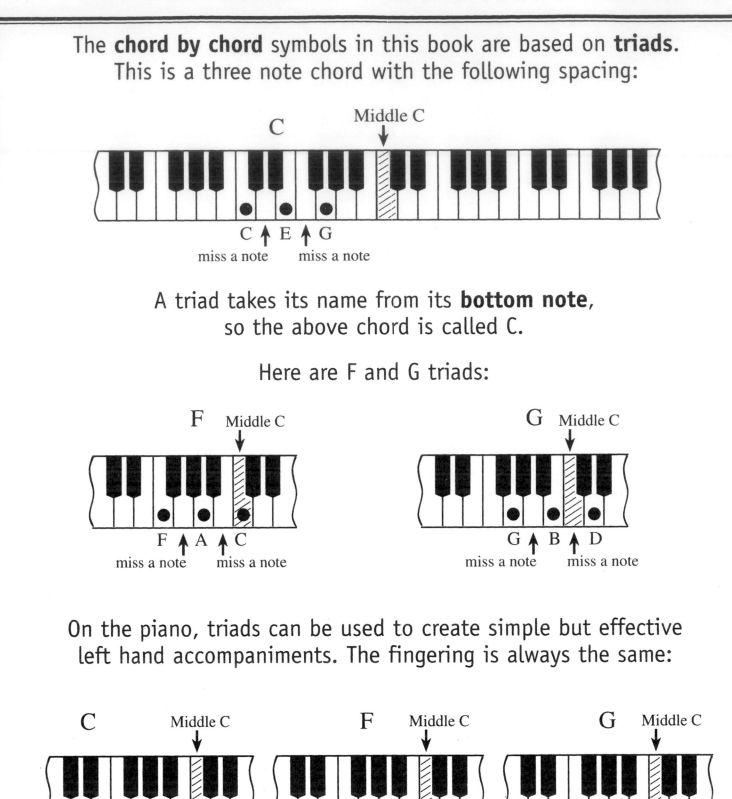

A triad takes its name from its **bottom note**,
so the above chord is called C.

Here are F and G triads:

On the piano, triads can be used to create simple but effective
left hand accompaniments. The fingering is always the same:

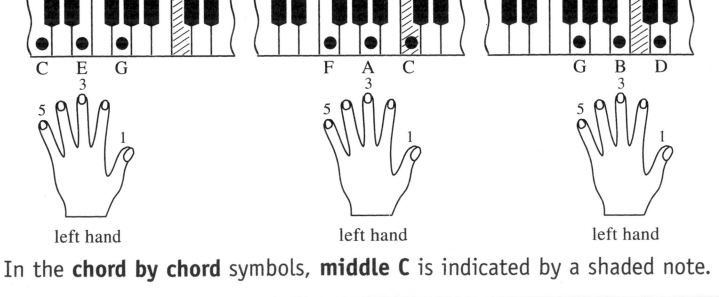

In the **chord by chord** symbols, **middle C** is indicated by a shaded note.